Daniel has been raised u[p] ... [ ]
seen hundreds hang on eve[ry] ... [ ]
sages. They run to the cross. He is a spiritual marksman. His
target is the heart. His arrows are sharp. His aim is perfect.
This book is a must-read!

—THE LATE EVANGELIST STEVE HILL
FOUNDER, HEARTLAND WORLD MINISTRIES CHURCH

These stories of revival are absolutely riveting. Many times I
found myself in tears, especially when reading the account of
the Brownsville Revival. I was there and played a role backing
my husband, Steve, in prayer as he prepared a new message
each and every day. It is exciting to read what God has done,
and I pray it stirs all of us to desire more!

There is a price to be paid for revival. To pursue more of the
Lord, there must be a dying of self. As the Word says, if we
seek Him we will find Him, if we search for Him with all our
heart (Jer. 29:13). It is obvious that Daniel has caught a flame
from the Lord and now burns to see others experience and
participate in that "trail of fire."

—JERI HILL
PRESIDENT, STEVE HILL MINISTRIES

WARNING: This book will provoke you! *Trail of Fire* is a contagious collection of timeless stories from a man whose heart
burns for revival. As you read these accounts of outpourings
that changed the world, Holy Spirit history will repeat itself in
your own life and ministry. The masterpiece Daniel Norris has
written is a catalyst that will make you hungry for revival and
leave you praying, "Do it again, God!"

—DANIEL KOLENDA
PRESIDENT AND CEO, CHRIST FOR ALL NATIONS
AUTHOR, *LIVE BEFORE YOU DIE*

Rarely, if ever, have I found myself more pressed into the heart
of Father than when reading the accounts of revival fire in
Trail of Fire by my friend Daniel Norris. This book does not
just possess profound truth, but it also presents the reality that
through hunger, holiness, expectation, and perseverance we
might once again experience a mighty outpouring! I challenge

you to read a chapter, then pray; read a chapter, then pray; and so on until you finish! Without another great awakening we are ruined as a nation and world. Oh, that we would cry out as Jonathan Edwards did when he said, "Oh, God, stamp eternity on my eyeballs!" This book is destined to be a map and a mandate for those crying, "More, Lord!"

—PAT SCHATZLINE
AUTHOR, *I AM REMNANT* AND *UNQUALIFIED*
EVANGELIST, REMNANT MINISTRIES INTERNATIONAL

Never have we lived in such need of revival as we do today! Neither has the church shown less interest in revival than it does today. One reason for such indifference is that few have ever experienced true revival and therefore don't understand how *essential* it is. Revival is God invading every aspect of our lives so that we never again return to mediocrity. My hope is that as you read these amazing incidents of revival, you will not only understand revival but will also experience it personally. Once you experience it, others will come and watch you *burn*. It's then you know you have experienced true revival.

—DAVID RAVENHILL
AUTHOR, *SURVIVING THE ANOINTING*

The path once trodden by courageous pioneers is easily missed by the overgrowth of indifference to our own history. Daniel Norris in his newest book, *Trail of Fire*, has begun to uncover stories that must be told. This trail marks the way for the many who will follow. I heartily recommend this book. You may very well discover guiding principles for your own journey.

—RICK CURRY
EVANGELIST, RICK CURRY MINISTRIES

Many have enjoyed the fire of revival but failed to maintain that fire. Daniel Norris, however, was consumed by the fire of revival and will forever burn with passion for God's presence. *Trail of Fire* honors the seasons of supernatural revival throughout history and will ignite your spirit with a hunger and passion for a move of the Spirit that is desperately needed and surely on its way!

Lord, please send Your revival fire once again!

—RICHARD CRISCO
PASTOR, ROCHESTER CHRISTIAN CHURCH

Daniel K. Norris

TRAIL
of
FIRE

CHARISMA
HOUSE

Most CHARISMA HOUSE BOOK GROUP products are available at special quantity discounts for bulk purchase for sales promotions, premiums, fund-raising, and educational needs. For details, write Charisma House Book Group, 600 Rinehart Road, Lake Mary, Florida 32746, or telephone (407) 333-0600.

TRAIL OF FIRE by Daniel K. Norris
Published by Charisma House
Charisma Media/Charisma House Book Group
600 Rinehart Road
Lake Mary, Florida 32746
www.charismahouse.com

Cover design by Vincent Pirozzi
Design Director: Justin Evans

Visit the author's website at www.danielknorris.com.

Library of Congress Cataloging-in-Publication Data:
Names: Norris, Daniel K., author.
Title: Trail of fire / Daniel K. Norris.
Description: First edition. | Lake Mary, Florida : Charisma House, 2016. |
    Includes bibliographical references.
Identifiers: LCCN 2016008450| ISBN 9781629986821 (trade paper) | ISBN
    9781629986838 (e-book)
Subjects: LCSH: Evangelists--Biography. | Revivals--History.
Classification: LCC BV3780 .N67 2016 | DDC 269--dc23
LC record available at http://lccn.loc.gov/2016008450

First edition

16 17 18 19 20 — 987654321
Printed in the United States of America

This book is dedicated to the intercessors of revival. You bear the burden of revival upon your knees. We are indebted to the prayers you have offered in the dark of night. Know that the greatest move of God now lies ahead.

CONTENTS

ACKNOWLEDGMENTS

To my amazing wife, Jenna—not only are you an amazing editor and partner in ministry, but you are also the love of my life. Thank you!

Grateful appreciation to Steve and Jeri Hill—you will be remembered among God's generals! Thank you for being a Paul to this Timothy.

A special thank-you to Maureen Eha, Debbie Marrie, and the team at Charisma—your belief in me and your hard work over the past few years have been a great encouragement.

To Heartland, thank you for persisting in prayer and contending for revival. No doubt Steve's heart and passion for revival has left a mark on us all. Each one of us is part of his legacy. The greatest days are ahead!

Finally, to our ThreeHundred—thank you for believing in this ministry and message. Together we are making big things happen!

I remember the days of old;
I meditate on all Your works;
I consider the work of Your hands.
I stretch forth my hands unto You;
my soul thirsts after You as a thirsty land. Selah

—Psalm 143:5–6

Introduction

A FIRE BEGINS

THERE IS NOTHING like a good story. Stories have the ability to ignite and inspire something deep within us. A good story is like a spark that hits the soul, stirs the imagination, and encourages us to believe that something extraordinary is possible. Stories are powerful! Is it any wonder that our story is part of the arsenal through which we overcome? As Scripture states, "They overcame him by the blood of the Lamb and by the word of their testimony, and they loved not their lives unto the death" (Rev. 12:11).

Life itself is a continual story that at this moment is still being written. It is a story lived by moments, not minutes. These moments capture the essence of who we are, where we come from, and inspire us toward what is possible. Every day invites a new opportunity for fresh experiences with the Lord. Stories are our way of sharing these moments and even encouraging one another in our individual journeys.

This is why the late Steve Hill, the evangelist from the Brownsville Revival, would invest hours with me in his office. He took time to pour into this hungry soul the stories of revival. He didn't just talk about what he had personally seen God do. He also shared the stories of great moves of God from the past. He knew that if people could capture a burning ember from one of these historic fires, it would ignite a fresh fire within their spirit. Such a flame, let loose into the world, might just start another great awakening—a greater awakening!

Steve was a student of revival history. He had a massive library filled with more than three thousand books. Very few were written in his own lifetime. They were all hard-bound books with that familiar old book smell and pages that had yellowed with time. Every book was written by or about the great saints who had gone on before us. It was a library filled with what Steve called "dead men's brains." He said he liked "finished accounts." In other words, he pre-ferred the words of men and women of God whose lives had validated their message, those who finished well and left no question about the integrity of their faith or lifestyle. They didn't just do something that caught attention for a moment then fall into a moral failure. He wasn't interested in preachers who simply had their fifteen minutes of fame. He wanted to immerse himself in studying the saints who endured until the end—men and women whose words still carry great weight and are just as relevant as when they were first typeset in an old press.

Steve would talk about Jonathan Edwards, a man who set the nation's eyes upon eternity. His account set my imag-ination ablaze. I could see Edwards preaching in a dark church hall, lit with lanterns and candles. In my mind's eye, the room was filled with anxious people crowded onto old wooden pews. As Edwards would preach, the listener would be spellbound by this man of God's message.

Edwards likened his congregation to a spider suspended over the fires of hell scarcely holding on by a single thread. The effect was striking. The message pierced their hearts and brought about a holy fear. Grown men and women began to dig their fingernails into the pews in front of them, clawing and clinging as if they were hanging on for their lives. Such images don't easily leave your mind! Hearing stories like that makes me wonder where such preaching has gone today. And it inspires me to believe that if God did it back then, He can do it again!

Steve's favorite preacher was a young, short, frail man from Scotland named Robert Murray McCheyne. The town called him "Holy McCheyne" because of the devoted life he lived before the people. His message was holiness, and he preached it hardest to himself. Steve said McCheyne would often walk through the town and crouch outside the windows of his parishioners' homes to listen in on their conversations at the dinner table. Intrusive? Perhaps, but they loved him for it. He was their pastor, and as such he constantly inspected the condition of his flock. Ultimately he led them to a place where a genuine revival of holiness would shake not only their church but also their country. Perhaps the thought of a holy pastor outside our windows might do us some good too!

I imagine that is one reason Steve kept these books nearby. They served as a constant reminder that the men and women who wrote them were part of the great cloud of witnesses that surrounded him (Heb. 12:1) and were very much interested in how he would continue the story they helped write.

Some of the books in Steve's collection were more than 350 years old. The oldest was a first edition set of *Foxe's Book of Martyrs*. This set was heavy, stood tall, and was hardbound in leather. He showed the set to me more than once. He barely cracked open the cover because he didn't want to damage the binding. You had to hold these books with respect and take great care with each fragile page. He wanted me to see the hand-drawn depictions of martyrdom that solemnly greeted you on those first pages. "Look at what they did to them," he said. What I saw was truly haunting—horrible images from a sixteenth-century artist who tried as best he could to show the sacrifice of the early saints. It was important to Foxe that we understand what these forerunners of our faith had to endure. And it was important to Steve that I see it.

Nearby was another prized possession, William Gurnall's *The Christian in Complete Armour*. Leonard Ravenhill once gave this book to David Wilkerson, telling him it would revolutionize his life. Wilkerson received it gladly. After all, who would turn down anything offered from that great revivalist? Wilkerson said he put the book aside at first because it was too long, too wordy, and written in Old English. But later, out of curiosity, he scanned the first few pages. That was all it took to bring him to his knees. If you've ever wondered where Wilkerson's nation-shaking messages were born, here is a clue. Gurnall's book was likely a seedbed for those fires.

Steve's library was intentional. He modeled it after that of Leonard Ravenhill, who was a personal mentor to him. Leonard had even provided Steve with a list of books and authors he believed were must-reads. Steve searched out those old books in antique shops around the world. There is something to be learned in that. Steve's father in the faith provided his spiritual son with the resources that would keep his eyes and messages focused on what really matters.

Steve didn't just keep these artifacts on the shelf; he also had them around the room. He had a rotating carousel shelf that belonged to D. L. Moody and an old wooden pulpit from a Methodist church built in the 1800s. He didn't know its history, but he liked to imagine John Wesley or George Whitefield having preached behind it. Next to the pulpit was a large credenza hand carved out of dark wood. It belonged to Wilkerson. On each door of the credenza was a beautifully carved lion head, which seemed to silently watch over the study.

For Steve collecting these items wasn't about trying to relive the past but about honoring it. He understood that they reflected the lives of great men and women who had run their race and finished well. These individuals are the ones who now cheer us on as we run ours. Remembering them helped encourage Steve as he ran his leg of the race. They inspired him to keep his eyes on the finish line. Is it any wonder God used him as He did?

WHERE ARE THE ELISHAS?

One afternoon I found myself sitting next to Steve as he was walking through what he called his "dark night of the soul." This was when he had been given up for dead. His doctors had encouraged him to enter hospice care and offered no hope to cure the cancer that had been attacking his body. He was resting, and I was there in case he needed anything. Sitting on the nightstand next to him was a book filled with stories from the Azusa Street Revival. I picked it up and started thumbing through the pages.

These were stories I had never heard. They were eyewitness accounts of the cloud of God's presence that never lifted and the amazing miracles that would take place each night during that revival. It stirred me to see how God used ordinary people to do such extraordinary things. As I read the stories, something happened in me. Tears welled up in my eyes and streamed down my cheeks. I couldn't help but take note of the setting where I found myself. Here I was sitting next to this great revivalist whom God had used to shake the world at the end of the twentieth century while reading stories from the revival that welcomed that century. These were the bookends of one hundred years of revival history. I was extremely grateful for all God had done, but I began to wonder what was to come. Would America experience another great revival? Could there be a place for me to serve in such a move? That afternoon my spirit began to burn anew for revival as I read the stories. There truly is power in a story!

The stories of revival are important. They are part of our shared history, and they are the reason we are where we are today. Steve understood that he was simply one part of a continuous trail of revival fire that had burned throughout history. It was passed from one person to the next as each ran his or her leg of the race.

Steve once asked me, "Do you understand what you are a part of?" He was referring to the spiritual trail of fire that men such as John Wesley, George Whitefield, Jonathan Edwards, Robert McCheyne, Andrew Murray, Charles Finney, William Seymour, Smith Wigglesworth, A. W. Tozer, and Leonard Ravenhill had blazed before me. He honored his spiritual lineage.

Does the contemporary church really understand what we are a part of? Truthfully, we don't. We don't know the stories of our past and have lost our connection to the ancient passion of these precious saints. My friend, this isn't about trying to live in the past, but about reclaiming the fires of those who have gone before us and igniting fresh ones in the present as we continue blazing the trail for the future. I believe God still has one last great awakening in store! He is looking for the ones who are willing to follow in the footsteps of the great men and women of God who have preceded us. He is looking for some Elishas—men and women of God who will pick up the mantles of departed generals and move forward to the next great awakening. Where are those Elishas?

On the day Elijah was taken up to heaven in that fiery chariot, his mantle fell from heaven. Elisha was there to pick it up. Elisha took it and asked, "Where is the LORD, God of Elijah?" (2 Kings 2:14). The answer to that question is one we already know. God is exactly where He has always been—on His throne. Not once has He ever vacated it. He has always been there and always will be. Writing about 2 Kings 2:14, Leonard Ravenhill asked a sequential and revealing question: "But where are the Elijahs of God?"[1] Where are His prophets, pastors, and people? For they are not where they should be.

Ravenhill continues, "We know Elijah was 'a man of like passions as we are,' but alas! we are not men of like prayer as he was!"[2] We are not a people of prayer, presence, or power like he was. James 5:16 tell us, "The effective, fervent prayer of a righteous man accomplishes much." James then pro-

> My friend, this isn't about trying to live in the past, but about reclaiming the fires of those who have gone before us and igniting fresh ones in the present as we continue blazing the trail for the future.

vides Elijah as an example of what a man fully given to God can do. Elijah prayed effective, fervent prayers and accomplished much. He prayed and the heavens were shut (1 Kings 17:1). He prayed again and the heavens opened (1 Kings 18:1, 41). He called fire down onto the altar and showed his nation who God was (1 Kings 18:16–40). James presents Elijah as a person in whose footsteps we can follow. He was like us, but are we like him?

Ravenhill wrote: "We love the old saints, missionaries, martyrs, reformers: our Luthers, Bunyans, Wesleys, Asburys, etc. [To that list I'll add our Finneys, Wigglesworths, Ravenhills, Wilkersons, and Hills.] We will write their biographies, reverence their memories, frame their epitaphs, and build their cenotaphs. We will do anything except imitate them. We cherish the last drop of their blood, but watch the first drop of our own!"[3]

Ravenhill asked, "Where are the Elijahs of God?" Honestly, we know the answer to that question as well. These are the heroes of the faith who have gone on before us. They are the men and women whose stories we love to share. Their lives burned brightly for the Lord. I now wonder if there is a man or woman today who is willing to follow in the footsteps of these modern Elijahs. Where are the Elishas of God? Where are the men and women of God who are willing to take up the mantles of those who have gone before us and walk in the Spirit as they did? Where are the young prophets who are bold enough not only to be inspired by the lives of these faithful saints but to imitate them as well? Where are the Elishas of God?

COMMON MAN, UNCOMMON ACTS

Elisha was a common man but capable of uncommon things. When we are first introduced to Elisha, we find him behind a plow. (See 1 Kings 19:19–21.) He is being faithful in the little things. He has diligently been working at the task he was assigned to do. Anyone who has ever worked behind a wheel, a desk, a phone, a keyboard, or a workbench understands the place where Elisha is. He was simply a common man working a common task.

Suddenly Elijah comes from behind and throws his mantle over Elisha's body. The Spirit of the Lord came over Elisha in that moment, and he suddenly got a glimpse of a different destination. For Elisha, this was when the fire first took hold of him. One moment all he could see was the end of that furrow he was trying to plow; in the next he sees a heavenly vision of a supernatural call. Elisha comes to the sudden realization, "There is more to life than the furrow I have been plowing. God has so much more for me to do!" That moment can come to you as well—when you realize there is more to life than the current ditch you've been digging. There is more to life than just earning a paycheck so you can pay another bill. Don't you yearn for more? My friend, it's time to let fresh fire from God touch you as well!

Elisha wastes no time. He calls out to the man of God and asks him to wait. He then slaughters his ox and burns his plow. At that moment we are invited to see what kind of man or woman God is looking for. He lets go of the old life to embrace the new. He burns the plow and slaughters the ox. There is no returning. He is not coming back to this place. Quitting would never be an option. Elisha was all in! This was Elisha's first uncommon act.

Oh, what glory is possible not only when God takes hold of a man, but also when the man takes hold of God! God can't use the self-sufficient. He uses the empty. He passes over the prideful and finds the humble. He is in search of the poor in spirit. The people who make themselves fully available to God always find that God makes His kingdom fully available to them. If God was looking for a king, or a man with unlimited resources, then we are all disqualified. He is not looking for our ability but our availability. For that we can all be candidates. Where are these Elishas?

Elisha set out to pursue the fire that had touched his life in that field. He followed in the footsteps of his spiritual father. Even when Elijah directed Elisha to stay behind in a place of safety or comfort, Elisha persisted in his pursuit. Three times the prophet told him to stay: "Stay here, please, for the Lord has sent me on to Bethel"; "Elisha, stay here, please, for the Lord has sent me on to Jericho"; "Stay here, please, for the Lord has sent me on to the Jordan." (See 2 Kings 2:2, 4, 6.)

Three times Elijah tries to leave his spiritual son behind, and three times Elisha refuses to stay put (2 Kings 2:1–6). He pursues his father, and each time he expresses his total commitment, saying, "As the LORD lives, and as you live, I will not leave you" (2 Kings 2:2). He knew Elijah was going to depart and that someone would need to take up the prophet's mantle. Elisha was determined to be that one. He pursued it. Where are the pursuers?

Finally they come to the Jordan River and cross over into the wilderness. Elijah asks his spiritual son, "'Ask for something, and I will do it for you before I am taken away from you.' And Elisha said, 'Let a double portion of your spirit be upon me'" (2 Kings 2:9).

I've heard this passage preached many times, and almost always the true meaning of Elisha's request is missed. Elisha was not asking for twice the anointing. He was not seeking twice the miracles and manifestations. He was asking for the right of the firstborn. In Hebrew culture the right of the firstborn was very important. Not only would this son receive a double portion of the inheritance, but also he would be responsible to carry on in his father's absence. It was his task to carry on the family business, to tend to the property, and look out for the family.

Elisha was saying to his spiritual father, "Someone is going to have to carry on for you. Someone will have to stand in the gap for the nation and continue to prophesy the word of the Lord. I want to be that son."

Elijah's response to Elisha seems strange at first. He says, "You have asked for a difficult thing" (2 Kings 2:10). Was

Elijah saying he wasn't sure whether this could be done? Of course not. Elijah had already heard from the Lord. When he was in the cave at the mountain of God, the Lord told him to anoint Elisha to succeed him as prophet (1 Kings 19:16). He knew this was the God-ordained man to carry his mantle. Yet he still said, "You have asked for a difficult thing."

Perhaps this is the very reason Elijah instructed him to stay behind three times. I believe he was testing Elisha. He offered the prophet refuge in Gilgal, Bethel, and Jericho. These were all safe places. Yet the younger prophet continued to pursue the elder prophet into the wilderness. Elisha knew Elijah would be leaving him that day, and he refused to miss the mantle. He knew that when Elijah went up, the mantle would come down—and he was going to be there to pick it up.

Elijah also knew Elisha. He knew Elisha would follow him out to the wilderness, and there Elisha would ask a difficult thing. He had to test him to see if he was truly willing. Elijah had carried this mantle for some time. He knew the weight and burden of it. He knew how heavy this call was and that it was a *difficult thing* to carry. He wouldn't just throw it on a man who wasn't fully willing to accept it. He gave Elisha an opportunity to decide. Was the younger prophet willing to bear the burden? Would he accept this "difficult thing"?

Elisha's mind was made up the day he first felt that fire—he would pursue it all the way to the end. Now, as one general prepared to depart, having run his leg of the race, another man was ready to pick up the mantle and run the next leg of the race.

Elijah was taken up, and the mantle came down. Elisha then took up the fallen mantle and asked, "Where is the Lord, God of Elijah?" (2 Kings 2:14). The answer was immediately evident. The Spirit of Lord now rested on Elisha.

This is the first ascension directly mentioned in the Bible, and it is a shadow of things to come. Elijah ascends to heaven in a chariot of fire. As he was carried up, something came down. A mantle was left for a son to carry. Elisha rips apart his old clothes and takes on his father's garments. He is clothed with the Spirit of God. He carries great power and anointing.

The second ascension occurred nine hundred years later. It was forty days after the crucifixion, when the time came for our Lord to ascend back to heaven. Jesus told His disciples it was good for Him to go up, because He would send the Holy Spirit down (Acts 1:6–9). Jesus was going up, and again, something was coming down!

Ten days later the first Spirit-filled revival in history occurred. One hundred twenty believers were gathered in one place seeking the face of God. They waited in their spiritual wilderness. They pursued to the very end. Then something came down. He came as fire and rested upon each of them—not just one man, but every man and woman. Everyone got a flame of their own.

Jesus had finished the first leg of the race; now it was time to pass the torch to the next runners. Since that first day and for the next two thousand years that fire has been passed from one person to the next. It has been handed down from generation to generation and has grown brighter in the passing. Do you realize what you are a part of?

The stories of revival are not just tales of the past! They are part of your story. Oh, my friend, we are in a moment in history when there is something falling from heaven that we can pick up and run with. In the days of Elijah many sat at a distance and watched as one man picked up the mantle.

Today every son and daughter can pick it up and run with it. This fire is not something for a few; it is available to all.

Revival is not a thing of the past. It is a living, active fire, and it is ready to take hold of you at this moment. Revival isn't a season that comes and goes. It is the fullness of God's Spirit coming alive in you. That has no expiration date. Right now is the time, right here in the present, for an ember from these past moves of God to be set loose within your spirit.

I will forever cherish those moments with Steve in his office as he shared these stories of revival. They have become part of my life and have fueled my passion for a national awakening. This is my hope for you as well. I have endeavored to capture the spirit of those times with Steve and write them into a narrative that will do for you what Steve did for me. Each story is told in such a way as to give you an idea of what it was like to be in the midst of that move of God. My goal is not just to give the facts of revival history but to impart the fires of revival history. I have looked back at the details left to us in the accounts of eyewitnesses and then used my discretion to connect the dots with a plausible narrative that stays true to the history.

I pray these stories will spark a fire deep within you that burns until you are fully consumed. God is looking for some Elishas. He is looking for men and women who will pick up one of the burning mantles of the past and let it consume them in the present. Are you ready?

The Wrath of God is like great Waters that are dammed for the present; they increase more and more, and rise higher and higher, till an Outlet is given, and the longer the Stream is stopt, the more rapid and mighty is its Course, when once it is let loose.... If God should only withdraw his Hand from the Flood-gate, it would immediately fly open, and the fiery Floods of the Fierceness and Wrath of God would rush forth with inconceivable Fury, and would come upon you with omnipotent Power; and if your Strength were Ten thousand Times greater than it is, yea Ten thousand Times greater than the Strength of the stoutest, sturdiest Devil in Hell, it would be nothing to withstand or endure it.[1]

—Jonathan Edwards, 1741

Chapter 1

STAMP ETERNITY ON MY EYES

The Great Awakening

*It is a fearful thing to fall into the
hands of the living God.*

—Hebrews 10:31

July 8, 1741, Enfield, Connecticut

O H GOD, STAMP eternity on my eyeballs,"[2] Jonathan Edwards prayed. Surely the reverend must
have uttered those words a dozen times already as he rode
atop his horse. He was traveling thirty miles south from his
home in North Hampton through the Connecticut River
Valley to the town of Enfield. There he and a fellow minister named Eleazar Wheelock were set to preach a series
of meetings.[3]

As Edwards rode alongside the river, eternity was
weighing heavily on his mind. It always was. Eternity was
the constant focus of this thirty-seven-year-old preacher's
intercession, especially on this day as he entered the town of
Enfield. He didn't know it then, nor could he, but that day
was already marked for eternity—not only for the people of
Enfield but also for the United States as well.

Enfield was desperately in need of a spiritual awakening.

This once-small frontier settlement had grown quickly into a prosperous town. In many ways it suffered from the same condition as the rest of the colonies. Success is often a double-edged sword. It comes as a reward for hard work and perseverance yet invites its own share of problems. The people of Enfield had become complacent in their success and drifted away from the very foundations that brought them prosperity. They seemed to have little interest in the things of God.

This is what was bringing Edwards to Enfield. He and Wheelock were hoping to spread the fires of revival there. All year long revival had been breaking out across the river valley. Every town was experiencing a fresh move of God— every town, that is, except Enfield. For some reason this town had proven to be particularly resistant. Edwards and Wheelock were trusting that through persistent prayer and preaching, the town of Enfield might be saved.

As Edwards rode in on this particular afternoon, he was greeted by the familiar sounds of a bustling little New England town. Horseshoes and wagon wheels clapped and cracked upon the cobblestone and wood-planked roads. The sound of each step reverberated off the surrounding buildings. Dozens of townsfolk milled about conducting their daily business. It was a typical day, and little seemed out of the ordinary—that is, nothing aside from Edwards.

Edwards was a peculiar man who often attracted attention with his strange habits. As he rode into town, he didn't engage in the common pleasantries one might expect. He seemed to have no desire to waste words with small talk. He just stared off into the distance as if he were looking at something over the horizon. Some were put off by what appeared to be rudeness on the minister's part. What kind of man just goes about ignoring the people around him? A few suspected this stranger might be a bit off.

Truthfully Edwards wasn't being rude, nor was he out of his mind. He was just becoming more and more preoccupied with the reality of eternity with every passing second. In his pocket he kept a handful of precious stones he had come across on his journeys.[4] As he rode along, his hand would slip into his pocket, and he would run his thumb and index finger across each of the stones, feeling each facet. He would then choose one and take it from its hiding place. Holding it high in the air and in the light of the sun, he'd look through the gem. He would then move it around, pondering the different shades and illuminations the sunlight produced as it passed through the prism. As the stone sparkled upon his eye, he began to think of John's description of God's celestial throne room.[5]

This was how Edwards' mind worked. It was always moving, always imagining and meditating on the things of God. The preacher spent the majority of his days in prayer and study.[6] Even when on long trips like the one to Enfield, Edwards refused to take his mind off God.[7]

As Edwards arrived at the First Church of Christ, he found his friend Eleazar Wheelock surprised to see him. Wheelock wasn't expecting Edwards until later in the week but was glad he had come. Wheelock had already been in Enfield for a few days preaching there and in the neighboring town of Suffield. He had seen a significant outpouring in Suffield that morning. Enfield, however, was proving to be stubborn.[8]

Wheelock was excited to share the testimony about the earlier service with his friend. He said that by the end of the meeting, everyone was weeping and crying out in repentance. He wondered if Enfield might be next. Though Eleazar had planned on preaching that evening, he now thought it wise to take advantage of his friend's early arrival. Perhaps Jonathan Edwards could get the breakthrough that up until now seemed elusive.

Together the two ministers entered the church and found people were already waiting. The meetinghouse itself was a forty-year-old wooden structure that was large enough to hold more than five hundred worshippers. It was the second such meetinghouse built in town.[9]

The crowd that gathered seemed rather indifferent toward the ministers. Wheelock was taken aback by their lack of civility. Turning to Edwards, he mumbled, "Have they no decency?" Needless to say, his expectation level for the service was not high. Edwards, on the other hand, seemed unaffected by the crowd's apparent apathy. After all, his eyes were not upon the people but upon eternity. He hoped he might set their eyes there as well.[10]

Edwards sat down on a wooden pew in the front of the sanctuary and began looking through his leather satchel for a message. He always traveled with several well-written sermon manuscripts. He was a thoughtful man who put considerable amounts of time into his writings. There on that bench he began to thumb through them one by one. The same hand that just earlier had rifled through his pocket, feeling for precious gems, now mined through his sermons looking for a priceless message, one that might bring eternity into view.

Edwards could have chosen any of the dozens of messages, but his fingers seemed drawn to a particular manuscript. It was titled "Sinners in the Hands of an Angry God." He paused as he considered the message. He had only preached it once before to his own congregation in North Hampton. That time it fell on deaf ears and had no effect.

The message had sat idle ever since. However, this evening he felt compelled to take it out and share it once more.

As Edwards prepared himself, Wheelock called the meeting to order. He offered a short prayer and began to greet the people. Wheelock was a passionate man who engaged his audience with a great deal of emotion. He had become known as the "chief intelligencer of revival news" and loved to share stories of different revivals taking place throughout New England.[11] He spoke of Reverend George Whitefield, who had recently been in the area. He told about the large crowds that were coming out to hear the evangelist and how greatly they were affected. Wheelock mentioned the service in Suffield earlier that day and how the people had responded to the message. Still, the crowd was unmoved. If Wheelock had hoped to change the atmosphere in the room, he was failing. Turning to Edwards and finding the minister ready, he introduced his friend and the pastor from North Hampton, Reverend Jonathan Edwards.

Edwards solemnly rose from his seat and approached the pulpit with his manuscript in one hand, a lit candle in the other. The contrast between the two ministers was immediately apparent. Wheelock was loud and exciting; Edwards was much more subdued. He had a solemn face and wore sober clothing. He didn't seek to draw attention to himself but to the Lord.[12]

In his typical fashion, Jonathan Edwards wasted no time. He greeted the congregation with a few words and then offered his text for the message. It was Deuteronomy 32:35, which Edwards read aloud, "Their foot shall slide in due time" (KJV).

Edwards wasn't a loud or emotional preacher. Nor was he timid. He chose each of his words carefully and spoke with such precision that he commanded the attention of his audience. Within moments they fell captive to his smooth but convicting voice.[13]

Wheelock couldn't help but note Edwards's affect upon the church. "How had he done it?" he wondered to himself. It seemed as if Edwards had somehow hypnotized them. It was certainly a wonder to behold. The message itself went beyond anything he had ever heard his friend preach.

Edwards was an entirely different sort of preacher. He didn't employ the theatrics other ministers might. He didn't want to manipulate anyone's emotions or be criticized as doing such. He simply trusted the truth of his words to convey the emotion rather than allowing an emotional presentation to overshadow that truth. Though he spoke in a peaceful manner, his words themselves were sharp. They fell with great weight upon the minds of the audience. Like a skilled surgeon with his scalpel, the master orator had already begun his work.

He now reached the heart of his message: "The Bow of God's Wrath is bent, and the arrow made ready on the String; and Justice bends the Arrow at your Heart, and strains the Bow; and it is nothing but the mere Pleasure of God, and that of an angry God, without any Promise or Obligation at all, that keeps the Arrow one moment from being made drunk with your Blood."[14]

Oh, how painful his words were to the unrepentant! Their affect was like hot molten steel upon the flesh. The crowd flinched, but the preacher remained still behind the pulpit. He read straight from his notes, rarely lifting his head. The few times he did look up, he stared toward the back of the room to one fixed spot. It was only then, by the glow of the candle on the podium, that you could see the tears that flowed from his eyes.[15]

He continued, "The God that holds you over the Pit of

Hell; much as one holds a Spider or some loathsome Insect over the fire, abhors you, and is dreadfully provoked; his Wrath towards you burns like Fire; he looks upon you as worthy of nothing else but to be cast into the Fire; he is of purer Eyes than to bear to have you in his Sight; you are Ten thousand times so abominable in his Eyes as the most hateful venomous Serpent is in ours."[16]

The impact of these words now brought a frightening revelation upon the room. The men and women who gathered that day—religious, backslidden, and worldly— suddenly realized they were each horribly doomed. They winced as if in great pain and discomfort. Some could no longer hold back the tears and began to weep. Even still, Edwards continued to press: "You have offended him infinitely more than ever a stubborn Rebel did his Prince; and yet 'tis nothing but his Hand that holds you from falling into the Fire every Moment."[17]

The stillness and the quietness in the room broke. People began to moan and cry out from their seats. One shouted to the minister, "What must I do to be saved?" Others screamed as if they feared for their very lives.[18]

Edwards paused to quiet the crowd. Once he had regained their attention, he continued: "'Tis to be ascribed to nothing else, that you did not go to Hell the last Night...but that God's Hand has held you up: There is no other Reason to be given why you han't gone to Hell since you have sat here in the House of God, provoking his pure Eyes by your sinful wicked Manner of attending his solemn Worship; yea, there is nothing else that is to be given as a Reason why you don't this very Moment drop down into Hell. O Sinner! Consider the fearful Danger you are in."[19]

A woman yelled to the preacher, "Oh, I am going to hell! What shall I do for Christ?"[20] Edwards stopped again and asked for silence, but to no avail. The shrieks and cries continued to grow as the preacher continued to ask for their attention. The commotion in the room had reached a fever pitch. Cries and shouts of sheer terror filled the room and were heard throughout the surrounding streets.

Many had taken a firm hold of their seats for fear of falling straight through the floor. They were convinced they were sliding down into the pits of hell itself. They clawed at the pews in front of them, digging their nails deep into the wood. Others clung to one another like a man drowning in deep water. Some fell to the ground as if they were brought down by an axe laid to their feet. They lay motionless upon the floor. Those who once stood now clung to the posts of the church believing the ground beneath them was giving way.[21]

Enfield had finally been humbled. Somehow this stoic preacher had done what others could not. So effective was his message that when he came to his close, he could not finish the sermon. His heaven-inspired words had cut so deeply that the people needed individual attention. He abandoned the pulpit and enlisted the other ministers in the room to console the grieving congregation. One by one they prayed with those who mourned until they found relief at the glorious cross.[22]

The meeting continued late into the night. As the hours passed, the atmosphere in the room slowly shifted. The weeping and groaning gave way to peace as each soul met Christ's saving grace. Once the congregation was once again under control, Wheelock closed out the meeting with a familiar hymn before dismissing with prayer.[23] Revival had come to Enfield.

A REVELATION OF ETERNITY

That night as the service concluded, Edwards knew that eternity had profoundly affected the town of Enfield. What he couldn't see was how that night was also destined to set eternity upon the eyes of a nation.

News about the revival in Enfield began to spread like a flame across paper. Copies of Edwards's message were quickly printed and distributed across all the colonies. Multiplied thousands were now able to read and experience the same message that so greatly affected Enfield. "Sinners in the Hands of an Angry God" caused a great turn in the preaching in America. Though it was not Edwards who ignited the Great Awakening, it was Edwards and more specifically this message that helped spread the fires of awakening far and wide.

How is it that a humble, solemn man like Edwards was used to move an entire nation to awakening? It's simple—he had eternity set before his eyes!

Steve Hill, the late evangelist who for many years led services in what became known as the Brownsville Revival, wrote of Edwards: "It is said that since his day no one merely possessing an eloquent touch and skilled mind could make such an impression from the pulpit. Edwards spent more time with the Lord and his books than in the social gatherings of his congregation. Though offensive to some, it was perhaps this devotion that brought such an anointing to the pulpit."[24]

Edwards prayed, "Oh God, stamp eternity upon my eyeballs."[25] What might happen if you and I were so bold as to pray a similar prayer? What if you asked God to forever stamp eternity before you? How might each second of every day be affected if it was counted with eternity firmly fixed in view? What would change? I imagine a great deal.

The great revivalist Leonard Ravenhill, author of *Why Revival Tarries,* once said, "If God should stamp eternity or even judgment upon our eyeballs, I'm quite convinced we'd be a very different tribe of people."[26] How true!

Revival will always bring eternity into view. It focuses the present-minded individual on the eternal reality that awaits beyond death. Living with eyes fixed firmly on present things causes a person to become content with the status quo. Revival wakes the complacent from their slumber, lest they become a causality of their short-sightedness.

This is exactly where America was before the First Great Awakening. Edwards brought a revelation of eternity and awakened a sleeping nation. Oh, how this nation needs such a divine revelation again. America sleeps as she slips further into the dark abyss of sin. Open our eyes, God! Stamp eternity upon our eyes! Give us a revelation of eternity!

ETERNITY LEAVES NO TIME TO WASTE!

We treat time as if it is something we have an abundance of. Do we really have so much? Is there time to kill? Have you found an inexhaustible fountain of youth and now have plenty of time to waste? The man who says, "I'm just wasting time," doesn't appreciate how foolish the statement is, or how revealing. Time is not something we can afford to waste. It is far too precious—perhaps the most precious and perishable thing we possess. We can grasp it but for a moment before it slips away with each passing second. There is so little of it, and once it is spent, it is gone forever.

It has been said that what we do in life echoes throughout eternity. The truth is, what we do in life determines eternity. Each moment of your life is like a valuable coin. You can spend it however you wish, but once spent, it's gone forever. Unfortunately too many waste too much precious time on temporary things. Their lives have purchased little of eternal worth. Right now, in the present, that may not seem so serious. However, a day is coming when the full weight of these words will come bearing down.

Consider for a moment that first step into eternity. You breathe your last breath on this earth and at once

> Revival will always bring eternity into view.

you're through the door to eternity. Just one step in and suddenly everything has changed! That moment will be beyond overwhelming. In an instant your perspective will dramatically shift. Suddenly things that used to consume you will no longer matter. At the same time, thoughts you continually ignored will come rushing to the forefront of your mind.

Upon your arrival you realize you entered as a pauper. You brought nothing with you. All the things you labored so hard to accumulate in life are gone. All the earthly things that seemed important are suddenly insignificant. Your notoriety, your possessions, the accolades, and the bank account you constantly stressed over mean absolutely nothing. All you have are the memories of what you did with the little bit of time you were allotted. Will that be a moment to celebrate or dread?

My friend, it is going to be a terribly awesome day. You'll step into eternity, and there you will finally see things as they are, not as you thought they were. I tremble as I write this, just thinking about seeing heaven, not as I have imagined it to be, but as it truly is. To see the streets of gold, the celestial sea, and the throne of my King is beyond the wildest of dreams! We shall finally see Jesus in the fullness of His glory. None of us are prepared for how striking that moment will be. He is far greater than any mind could ever conceive.

The Apostle John wrote about this experience. He said: "I turned to see the voice that spoke with me.... The hair on His head was white like wool, as white as snow. His eyes were like a flame of fire. His feet were like fine brass, as if refined in a furnace, and His voice as the sound of many waters. He had in His right hand seven stars, and out of His mouth went a sharp two-edged sword. His appearance was like the sun shining brightly. When I saw Him, I fell at His feet as though I were dead" (Rev. 1:12, 14–17).

Think about this. John had known Jesus on the earth as the lamb who was slain, but in eternity he sees Him as He truly is—the lion who reigns. Until this point John had only seen Jesus in the flesh. He had walked with Jesus and laid his head upon Christ's chest. John was the disciple "Jesus loved" (John 13:23). If there was ever a man on earth who could say, "I know Jesus," it was John. However, in heaven John sees a much different Jesus than the one he knew on earth. Jesus, the son of God, is no longer veiled in the flesh. He is fully revealed as the awesome God He is. The fullness of His light shines so bright John falls like a dead man at His feet. Truly what a day that will be—an awesome, terrible, sobering day! The day we step into eternity is the day we see Jesus.

THIS DAY OR THAT DAY?

The sixteenth-century reformer Martin Luther said, "There are only two days on my calendar. This day and that day."[27] By *this day* he meant the life he was currently living, and by *that day* he was looking toward eternity when he would face a righteous Judge. Luther understood it is what we do with *this day* that makes a difference on *that day*.

It is tragic that eternity is something rarely talked about in the modern church. Much emphasis is placed on helping believers live a better life here on earth, yet little is said to prepare the saints for what comes after. Have we forgotten that one day every individual ever born will stand before God in eternity to be judged? Paul warns that we will all stand before God's judgment seat, and each of us will give an account of himself or herself to God (Rom. 14:10, 12).

That day for the sinner

Everyone will stand before Jesus one day and be judged. For those who have yet to surrender to Jesus, I am afraid that day will be a terribly frightening one. John saw it and painted a very fearsome picture:

> Then I saw a great white throne and him who was seated on it. The earth and the heavens fled from his presence, and there was no place for them. And I saw the dead, great and small, standing before the throne, and books were opened. Another book was opened, which is the book of life. The dead were judged according to what they had done as recorded in the books. The sea gave up the dead that were in it, and death and Hades gave up the dead that were in them, and each person was judged according to what they had done. Then death and Hades were thrown into the lake of fire. The lake of fire is the second death. Anyone whose name was not found written in the book of life was thrown into the lake of fire.
>
> —REVELATION 20:11–15, NIV

This is known as the Great White Throne judgment. John saw that "the earth and the heavens fled from his presence, and there was no place for them." Can you imagine this? Here is God Most High seated upon His throne. It is such a fearsome sight that even creation is terrified to touch Him. It refuses to get close to Him. The earth and sky roll away from His presence like a violent storm. Surely this is the "angry God" Edwards preached about. He is the Judge of judges, and the time has come to put the sinner on trial.

John writes that the dead, both "great and small" are summoned to the courtroom to stand before the Judge. All of history must come—no one will be exempt. That day the *great* will appear. Among them are the kings and leaders who once pompously exercised their authority upon the earth. Now they stand before the preeminent authority. They refused to humble themselves before God on earth, but here in His awesome presence they have no choice. Consider the irony that awaits these *great* leaders. What will it be like for Pontius Pilate on that day? The last time he saw Jesus, he sentenced Him to die on the cross. Pilate foolishly judged Jesus on earth, but Jesus will judge Pilate in eternity. I imagine on that day Pilate will wish he had been more discerning when he stood as judge.

Not only will the *great* appear, but also the *small*. Everyone who has not surrendered to Jesus will be brought before the throne. The library of heaven will be opened, and the sinner will be judged according to the record books. Trust me, not one thing will be missed. Every crime, every misdeed, and every evil thought will be lined up against the sinner. One by one they will be put in full view for all to see. The evidence will be overwhelming. There will be no defense. All will be judged according to God's perfect law. There will be no doubt the sinner is guilty, and the decision will be final. There can be no appeal.

The sinner will beg for mercy on that day, but the day for mercy will have passed. The opportunity was missed. Everyone whose name is not found in the book of life will be cast away from God's presence forever and subjected to eternal fire. My friend, these are hard words, but every one of them is true. That day will be a horrible day for those who do not know Christ.

It is a shame that Edwards's sermon is often portrayed as a fear-inducing, fire-and-brimstone message. Nothing could be further from the truth. Yes, the message is sobering and carries heavy words, but they were words filled with grace. Edwards didn't deliver them with anger but with tears. He had spent countless hours praying over each and every word. His message carried such weight because it came from a place of prayer.

Edwards was first and foremost a pastor, and just as a good shepherd should, he knew his flock well. He understood that, by and large, the problem facing Enfield and the rest of the colonies was not a lack of familiarity with the gospel. They were fully aware of the gospel remedy; they just didn't know the necessity of embracing that answer. "Sinners in the Hands of an Angry God" came like a firm slap to the face of a man asleep in the midst of grave danger. It stung for a moment but offered salvation for eternity.

I am often asked how a loving God could ever send anyone to a terrible hell. My answer is always the same. God doesn't send anyone to hell; each of us was already headed there when we were born. The Bible clearly teaches that "all have sinned and come short of the glory of God" (Rom. 3:23). It tells us that "there is none righteous, no, not one" (Rom. 3:10) and that "the wages of sin is death" (Rom. 6:23). The sinner chooses hell by embracing their sin and rejecting God.

Yes, God is a God of love, but He is also a God of justice. One day He will punish sin and those who choose to remain in sin. There is nothing trivial about sin. There is no such thing as just a little sin. All sin is already marked for punishment. As Edwards said, the bow of God's wrath is already bent toward it, ready to destroy it.[28]

But because God is gracious and loving, He went to the greatest lengths possible to rescue us from hell. He sent His Son, Jesus, to die a brutal death upon the cross so we might find life. Look at the cross, and you'll see the full extent of God's love.

This is where grace is found in "Sinners in the Hands of an Angry God." Yes, we are born into sin. Yes, God is angry with our sin. Yes, God's full wrath is bent toward sin and will soon destroy it. Yet it is His hands—the hands of an angry God—that hold us. We deserve His punishment, yet we find His protection. That is a radical thought worthy of much meditation. In that regard, this message may be the most grace-filled message ever preached.

There is a terrible day of judgment coming for the sinner, but you can escape it if you call on His name! Call on the name of Jesus and be saved. That is why He came. It is why He died—so you could enjoy everlasting life.

That day for the saint

As rare as it is to hear sermons today about the judgment of sinners, it is even rarer to hear about the judgment of the saints. Make no mistake: the Christ follower is not exempt from judgment. Paul wrote, "For we must all appear before the judgment seat of Christ, that each one may receive his recompense in the body, according to what he has done, whether it was good or bad" (2 Cor. 5:10).

At the judgment seat of Christ the believer is judged according to everything he or she has done *since* salvation. Every deed, every word, and every second of the person's life is going to be put to the test. That day will be a serious and solemn day as well.

Jesus calls us friends (John 15:15), but we must not forget

that He is the King of kings and Lord of lords. His eyes blaze with fire, and His feet glow as though He stands in a molten fire. When He speaks, His words flow with such force you feel as though all the water on earth is being poured upon you at once. (See Revelation 1:14–15.) What an awesome revelation of His reality will take place on that day!

On our judgment day every saint will appear to be judged for what he or she did while in this life. Paul cautions us to be careful how we build upon the foundation of Christ, or how we choose to live our lives:

> Now if anyone builds on this foundation with gold, silver, precious stones, wood, hay, or stubble, each one's work will be revealed. For the Day will declare it, because it will be revealed by fire, and the fire will test what sort of work each has done. If anyone's work which he has built on the foundation endures, he will receive a reward. If anyone's work is burned, he will suffer loss. But he himself will be saved, still going through the fire.
>
> —1 CORINTHIANS 3:12–15

On that day our Christian life will be tried by fire. We love to talk about His fire. We sing songs about His fire, but on that day, my friend, we shall see His fire. The Scriptures say that "our God is a consuming fire" (Heb. 12:29) and that He dwells in an "unapproachable light" (1 Tim. 6:16). Your life's work will be put in His fire, and everything will be exposed for what it really is.

The things that are worthless are represented by the wood, hay, and stubble. They stand no chance in the fire. They become ashes. Those things that are precious—the genuine works done before the Lord from a pure heart—will be revealed for the priceless treasures they are. Every work is put to the fire and judged, not just your actions but also your motives. Everything will be brought into light on that day. Nothing will be hidden. Those things done in secret will be revealed. There will be a full accounting for every deed. This is the final test! Will you pass through the fire and be rewarded? Or will you barely escape? As Ravenhill said of that day, pray that you're not standing knee deep in ashes![29]

Already I can hear someone saying, "Brother, you're talking about works." Yes, I am! I am because He is. Christ is very much concerned about your works—not because we are saved *by* works but because we were saved *for* works. As Paul stated, "We are His workmanship, created in Christ Jesus for good works" (Eph. 2:10).

I want to make something perfectly clear: what you believe about Christ and the cross determines *where* you will spend eternity, but it's what you did with Christ and the cross that will determine *how* you will spend eternity. We all must give an account for what we have done with the life Jesus gave us. We all must account for the time we spent here on earth as well as how we used the talents and opportunities God placed in our hands.

This is why we are cautioned to "be patient and stand firm, because the Lord's coming is near. Don't grumble against one another, brothers and sisters, or you will be judged. The Judge is standing at the door!" (James 5:8–9, NIV).

It's going to be a serious day! It's time we start to pray, *"Oh, God, stamp eternity on my eyes!"*

LIVING FOR ETERNITY

Do you see it now? We are not living for this day but for *that* day. It is the only day that matters. Eternity leaves no time to waste. What I do with this day I have been given determines what happens on that day. Until eternity comes into view, it is likely that precious time will continue to be wasted.

One of Edwards's "strange" habits was keeping a pocket full of precious stones. I say "strange" only because it seemed peculiar to the people who saw him. Edwards was one of the few in his right mind. A man with eternity in his eyes will always seem strange to the world around him. When everyone was living for the here and now, Edwards looked beyond. This is why he kept the gems close by. They were a reminder. When he lifted one before his eyes, he changed the lens through which he viewed the world.

Isn't that exactly what happens when God stamps eternity upon our eyes? He changes the lens through which we view the world. When eternity is lifted before us like a precious stone, we see the world differently. Suddenly things become crystal clear. The places we invest our time, the people with whom we spend time—everything is processed through that lens of eternity.

When our minuscule amount of time is weighed in the light of eternity, it forces us to wake up. There is no time to waste, not another moment to slumber. Too much is at stake! So are you willing to take the plunge? Are you daring enough to truly pray, "Oh, Lord, set eternity before my eyes!"? I hope so, because if you do, nothing will ever be the same.

The effects of this meeting through the country were like fire in dry stubble driven by a strong wind. All felt its influence more or less.... The whole country appeared to be in motion to the place, and multitudes of all denominations attended. All seemed heartily to unite in the work, and in Christian love. Party spirit, abashed, shrunk away. To give a true description of this meeting cannot be done; it would border on the marvellous. It continued five days and nights without ceasing. Many, very many will through eternity remember it with thanksgiving and praise.[1]

—Barton Stone, 1801

Chapter 2

FIRE ON THE FRONTIER

The Cane Ridge Revival

*I will remember the works of the LORD; surely I will
remember Your wonders of old. I will also meditate
on all Your work, and talk of Your deeds.*

—**Psalm 77:11–12**, NKJV

Friday, August 6, 1801, Cane Ridge, Kentucky

THE NARROW DIRT road to the log cabin church
house in Cane Ridge was crowded with hundreds
of wagons, carriages, horses, and even people on foot. It
seemed as if the whole countryside was literally descending
upon the church. Even as it continued to rain, making a
mess of the road, the people still came by the thousands.

The population of Cane Ridge was growing by the hour
as the fields around the church were transformed into a
new community made up entirely of tents. Some folks
had traveled over one hundred miles from as far as Ohio
and Tennessee. They came with their entire families and
arrived with their own provisions. It was an awesome sight
to behold, especially for Barton Stone, the pastor of the
Presbyterian congregation in Cane Ridge.[2]

This scene was somewhat reminiscent of the ancient

Israelites as they camped around Mount Sinai. There in the wilderness God met with His nation from within the fire (Exod. 19:18). Stone trusted that God would do the same in America's own wilderness. Just a few years before, a religious gathering like this was unheard of. Times had changed, and camp meetings were quickly becoming a popular means of meeting the spiritual needs of an expanding nation. On this day men and women, black and white, slave and free, were coming together to meet with God. It was apparent that something extraordinary was taking place.

The multitude had come in anticipation of a Communion service set to take place that Sunday. Reverend Stone had sent word far and wide that this would be "one of the greatest meetings of its kind ever known."[3] He did not plan to disappoint.

The United States was barely twenty-five years old, and Kentucky had just joined the Union less than ten years earlier. The new nation was quickly growing as more and more people continued to venture west. The days of Jonathan Edwards and the Great Awakening had already begun to fade as the nation expanded. Once again the moral foundations America once knew were slowly eroding. Churches were few and far in this vast land. As people moved farther and farther from churches, they began to forsake the Lord. This was the wild frontier, where the only rule of law was a gun or a rope. It was a time when wickedness abounded and very few people professed real faith.

Reaching such vast communities required churches to adopt a new approach. The distance made it impractical to expect people to come weekly or even monthly to a church house to partake of the Lord's Supper. Communion was an exercise that still carried great weight in the religious hearts of the people. The camp meeting was one way to help facilitate this.

Congregations sent word to neighboring farms and villages inviting all to share in the Lord's Supper. Since many had to travel a considerable distance to make it to church, they were invited to stay with families closer to the church or to camp on the grounds. In many ways, camp meetings were a natural complement to frontier living. They also provided a sense of community while giving families the opportunity to focus upon spiritual matters.

The camp meeting at Cane Ridge would have an opening service on Friday night, which would be followed by a day of fasting, prayer, and preaching on Saturday. Then on Sunday Communion would be given to all who wished to participate. Everyone was expected to break camp and head home by Monday.

Barton Stone had just started pastoring in Cane Ridge three years earlier.[4] He was a slender twenty-nine-year-old with dark, wavy hair that he kept short and always combed straight back. Stone had first heard about these camp meetings a year before. When it was announced that one would take place in Logan County in the spring, he made sure to attend.[5] It was a two-hundred-mile-journey south, but the trip was worthwhile. There were more than five thousand people in attendance. The scene was unlike anything he had ever witnessed. It made quite the impression on the young minister. He left that weekend and immediately began to plan to host one at Cane Ridge.

Stone expected a large crowd, a larger group than the church house could possibly hold. He would use the church for prayer and Communion, but the services themselves would have to be held outdoors in the adjacent field. Stone had a raised and covered platform constructed using timber from some of the nearby pine trees. He had also invited seventeen ministers from different denominations to help minister to the anticipated crowd. He felt prepared to meet the needs of all who would attend.[6]

As evening approached, the rain continued to pour, putting a damper on the opening service scheduled for that evening. Most of the people chose to remain inside the comfort of their tents. Some held their own prayer services with friends and family. Those who were brave enough to walk through the rain found safe harbor inside the church house. The crowd that evening was small enough to fit comfortably there.

The church was a tall log cabin. Inside there was a single room that was thirty feet by fifty feet. A balcony had been added along the back wall, and the left and right side to provide more seating. The church provided enough room for four hundred worshippers.[7] That night the house was full as Reverend Stone greeted the people. A message was delivered, and the people dismissed. The service itself was rather uneventful. It was the calm before the storm.

The sky had cleared by Saturday morning, and the first service took place from the covered platform that had been constructed outside the church. Thousands gathered there, and a tangible excitement could be felt in the air. The crowd continued to grow throughout the day. By the afternoon it was evident that there were far more people than any had anticipated. Where had they all come from? There were at least twenty-five to thirty thousand men, women, and children on the grounds! It became immediately apparent that neither the meeting house nor the raised platform would be adequate to minister to such a large crowd.[8]

Reverend Stone dispatched the preachers who had joined him to minister throughout the multitude. It was an awesome display of humility and unity. Presbyterian, Methodist, and even some Baptist preachers set out into the fields to contend for a harvest amongst the people. Stumps, carriages, or fallen trees became platforms for the preachers as they ministered to different sections of the crowd. Sometimes as many as eight different ministers would be preaching at a single time, yet there was no confusion.[9] The message was salvation through faith. The call was to repent of worldly and wicked ways, turning to Jesus Christ as the only way to the Father. So many heeded the call to salvation they were unable to count them all.

In the crowd that afternoon was a mother standing with her two teenage daughters at her side. They were listening to a minister who stood before them on a stump. He preached with powerful words about the deadly consequences of sin. As they listened, the two daughters were suddenly seized with conviction. They cried out from the depths of their souls and then fell to the ground like two dead women.

This was a new sight for everyone in the crowd. The mother, a devout woman who loved the Lord, became quite distressed. She began to franticly fan their faces in an attempt to wake them up, but to no avail. It was an hour later when one of her daughters stirred just long enough to cry out with a piercing scream, "Mercy, Lord! Mercy!" She then fell back into her trancelike state. Both girls lay there motionless for hours upon the ground with the most awful look of terror upon their faces. From time to time they would wake just enough to cry out for mercy once more before returning to their agonizing slumber.[10]

The wretched despair they carried on their countenance lasted for a few hours, before it finally broke. It was replaced with the most beautiful, heavenly smile. "Precious Jesus!" one shouted as she rose to her feet. The whole of her being

had been transformed. She was filled with such fire and zeal
that containing it was impossible. She opened her mouth
and began to preach the gospel to all those who surrounded
her. Her voice belted across the crowd as if it were amplified
with a supernatural force. It caused a stir, and a new crowd
began to gather around.[11]

All across the camp similar scenes were taking place.
People would flock around anyone who had taken a position to preach. At first it was the ministers, but as the
congregation began to be affected, many others rose up
to share. It was not uncommon to see a man or woman
struck down to the ground just as the two young ladies
had been and then rise up with an intense urge to preach.
These untrained ministers suddenly declared the wonders
of God. Their appeals were eloquent, solemn, bold, and
free. When they would preach, people would gather and
oftentimes many of those would be flung to the ground
themselves. Sometimes they would fall by the hundreds
all at once. They hit the ground like trees felled by one
swing with a powerful axe.[12]

It was a strange sight to Barton Stone. Men and women
were falling everywhere, taken down as men slain in battle.
Bodies lay everywhere and would remain motionless upon
the ground for hours. That is, until they were stirred to life
with deep groans or shrieks. All over the fields you could
hear the desperate cries and calls for mercy from thousands
at a time.

Falling was just one of the peculiar manifestations that
took place that day. As evening approached, many found
themselves unable to control their bodies. Someone called
these strange actions "the jerks," and the name seemed
appropriate. Sometimes it would affect just a head or an
arm or a leg, and the body part would twitch or jerk in the

most unusual fashion. A few had these movements take over their entire bodies. One man was seen bending so far forward that his head nearly touched the ground; then he would bend just as far backward. Strange as it may seem, not a single person complained that these jerks caused them any discomfort.

Some found it a humorous sight, especially those who came to criticize or mock. In the crowd was a local physician who had come to Cane Ridge out of curiosity. The scene was inexplicable to his analytical mind. He joked to a young woman that should he become affected, she would have to make sure he didn't hurt himself on his way to the ground. As he mocked, he became more and more uncomfortable. Soon it was too much for him to handle. The man tore off into the woods, running for his life. He didn't make it far before he too was struck down. He lay there on the ground until he fully submitted his life to the Lord.[13]

As the sun set that night, preaching continued to be heard throughout the camp. Periodically the crowd would be moved to sing a familiar hymn. It would start at one end of the camp and then move like a wave throughout the entire multitude. The sound of thousands of voices singing in the open air had a powerful effect on many. It flowed like a mighty torrent throughout the surrounding hills. The singing seemed to come not from the mouth but from the very depths of the soul. Such music silenced everything and attracted everyone's attention. It was a heavenly sound no one ever tired of hearing.[14]

The meeting on Saturday had exceeded Stone's prediction. Though the services were set to conclude on Sunday, few wished to leave. The meeting continued through the

following week and might have gone longer had the crowd
not have exhausted the resources of the town.[15]

Word spread quickly about the meeting at Cane Ridge.
As a result, more and more camp meetings began to spring
up across America's frontier. Though none ever matched
the attendance of Cane Ridge, the impact they made on
America was significant. Each camp meeting that took
place after Cane Ridge began with a similar prayer, "Lord,
make it like Cane Ridge."[16]

LORD, DO IT AGAIN, LIKE CANE RIDGE!

The story of Cane Ridge is one that seems too spectacular
to be true. Had it not been for the many eyewitnesses who
recorded the event in great detail, it might be easy to dismiss it as a tall tale. There is no denying that something
supernatural took place in the cane fields of Kentucky. The
camp meeting shook several denominations, including
the Presbyterians, Methodists, and Baptists. This revival
ignited a fire that swept through the Western frontier like
a wildfire through dry bush. It set the stage for America's
next great awakening. Barton Stone testified, "To give
a true description of this meeting cannot be done; it
would border on the marvellous.... Many, very many
will through eternity remember it with thanksgiving and
praise."[17]

The story of the Cane Ridge revival is one that stirs something deep within the spirit. Every year thousands of people
still make the trek to Cane Ridge, Kentucky, to visit that
old log cabin meeting house. They go to learn about and to
remember this remarkable move of God. Some go in hopes
of capturing a burning ember of that ancient fire. All leave
with the same prayer resounding in their hearts, "Lord, do
it again, like Cane Ridge!"

Oh, that God would do it again and do it like Cane Ridge! Oh, that He might visit this land with such a move of His Spirit that is so awesome it shakes sinners and stirs saints! Barton Stone described the nation before Cane Ridge like this: "So low had religion sunk, and such carelessness universally had prevailed, that I have thought that nothing common could have arrested the attention of the world."[18] Revival came as a much-needed answer from heaven.

We find our nation in this place once again. The faith of many has sunk low, and worldliness has invaded not only the land but the church as well. America once again needs something uncommon to burn through the dry brush. We desperately need revival.

The psalmist Asaph wrote, "I will remember the works of the LORD; surely I will remember Your wonders of old. I will also meditate on all Your work, and talk of Your deeds" (Ps. 77:11–12, NKJV). There is great benefit in looking back at the stories of the past to be encouraged by all God has done. Especially in times of great darkness or spiritual drought, these stories remind us that we've been here before, and when we finally turn back to God, He always revives.

In this passage from Psalm 77 the psalmist was recalling the marvelous wonders God performed in the desert. God met with His people in the wilderness with fire, smoke, thunder, and lightning (Exod. 19:16–18). Time and time again God delivered Israel from the hands of the enemy and miraculously provided for them in a desert wasteland. Asaph saw the wisdom of looking back and remembering the past moves of God.

Asaph was King David's chief musician. Stop and think about that for a moment. Asaph was David's worship leader. David was a celebrated musician himself, a man after God's own heart, the one from whose bloodline the Messiah would come. What kind of man would David choose to be his chief musician, the one responsible for leading continual worship before the Lord? For Asaph to have been in that role, he undoubtedly was a man who carried the heart of two kings—a natural one and an eternal one.

> If revival tarries, it is because we have been reluctant to tarry before the Lord.

History tells us that Asaph was there the day the ark of the covenant was brought back into Jerusalem. It had remained outside the city for years. David jealously longed for the day it would be returned. Finally that day arrived, and with it came celebration and national revival. This was the day Asaph was appointed to lead worship continually before the ark (1 Chron. 15:16–17). What a powerful moment this must have been for Asaph!

However, over time something changed. Asaph found himself in great distress. From the very depths of his soul he said, "I cried out to God with my voice, even to God with my voice; and He listened to me. In the day of my trouble I sought the Lord; in the night my hand is stretched out and does not weary, my soul refuses to be comforted" (Ps. 77:1–2).

It is not entirely clear exactly what Asaph was lamenting about. However, his words let us know he was experiencing a time of great affliction, and he could find no relief by day or rest at night. He cried out to the Lord, and it appeared as if God had not answered. Asaph inquires, "Will the Lord cast off forever, and will He be favorable no more? Has His mercy ceased forever, and have His promises failed for all time? Has God forgotten to be gracious, and has He in anger shut up His tender mercies?" (Ps. 77:7–9).

Of course, the answer to these questions is a resounding, "No!" Asaph knew this truth well. Still, he couldn't help but wonder why the answer tarried. Asaph's affliction brought the man of God to his knees. When in great distress, he had no choice but to call upon the Lord for an answer.

If revival tarries, it is because we have been reluctant to tarry before the Lord. It is true that as long as we remain content to live without revival, we will continue to remain without revival. However, I believe that in this day God is beginning to unsettle some Asaphs. The rebellion of the land is producing a great affliction within our souls, and with each passing day we are growing more and more distressed. This divine affliction is bringing us, as lovers of God, to our knees to cry out, "Lord, do it again!"

The Cane Ridge revival marks a pivotal point in the history of our nation. The sins of the land continue to pile up. America has lost her way and forgotten why she was founded. A great battle is raging for the soul of the nation. Just as it did before Cane Ridge, America again has moved away from the godly principles upon which we were founded. We desperately need another move of God!

Where are the modern-day Asaphs who will weep and wail through the night over America's great apostasy? Where are those who will stand between heaven and earth and contend for mercy upon our land? Where is the church at this hour, when she is needed the most? It is time to wake up from our slumber and pray through the night, calling out, "Lord, do it again, like Cane Ridge!"

The sad reality is the modern-day church is failing this nation. That is a strong statement, but it is no less true. Yes, we live in a time when it seems the church is enjoying a season of success. Our churches have never been larger and never had more at their disposal, yet we see so few results.

To some it may appear that the church is doing quite well. Multiple megachurches populate every major city. They draw crowds of thousands each weekend. Our sanctuaries are adorned with the latest technology. We have perfected our programs and processes. Church planting and church growth have been turned into simple, reproducible formulas. Yet with all that we can boast about, our communities and nation remain unaffected.

It is estimated that more than 150,000 people walk out of church each week never to return.[19] That figure is not for each year, but each week! That totals eight million people a year who walk out the back door and into an uncertain eternity. Christianity in America is not in a state of incline but decline. This alone should sound the alarm. One church may grow, but it does so at the expense of another that shrinks. Moving believers from smaller buildings into one larger facility may make it look like a congregation is growing, but those changes haven't impacted the kingdom. Satan does not fear a church that can fill a large hall; he fears a church that can empty hell.

A recent study showed that the number of Christians in America shrank by 7.8 percent over the course of just seven years.[20] That was the largest drop ever recorded in the nation's history. If things hold true, that number is likely to double in the next seven years. Whatever growth we celebrate within our churches is not keeping pace with our rapidly changing nation. Please hear this: without a seismic shift in our churches, you and I will one day experience a future in which the church has become irrelevant in our culture. It's time to wake up! It's time to call the Asaphs to pray. We need revival in America again!

Take a moment to consider just how low the religious culture of the nation has truly sunk, and ask yourself, "Where are the Asaphs who are afflicted by this nation's great sin?"

Where are the Asaphs who will lament the loss of three thousand babies each and every day? The number of children denied the right to life has reached fifty million and is rising.[21] These babies are slaughtered in the name of choice and convenience. That is two children every minute who are ripped apart limb by limb from their mother's womb. If the blood of one man cries out from the ground for justice (Heb. 12:24), what must the blood of fifty million innocent children sound like?

Where is the anguish in the church concerning abortion? Where is the collective outcry from the pulpits, calling out the atrocities and mobilizing us to action? How can we continue to sleep in a land that slaughters the most innocent? God will not hold us blameless in this hour. Silence in the face of evil is itself evil. We need revival in America again!

Where are the Asaphs who will weep through the night over the murder of Christians taking place at this moment all around the world? We have sat back and watched the rise of radical Islam in our day, which has caused millions of families to be displaced and tens of thousands to be martyred for the cause of Christ. How has this affected the church?

The world watched in horror as radical Muslims executed twenty-one Christians from the Egyptian church on the beaches of Tripoli. They were marched out in a single-file line, in orange prison uniforms. One by one they were forced to kneel in the tides of the Mediterranean as a masked man put a machete to their throat. Each was given a chance to renounce Christ and accept Muhammad as their prophet. When they refused, they were decapitated. Twenty-one men were martyred and their murders were videotaped and broadcast for the world to see.[22] How has this affected the church? How many prayer services have been organized to lift these families up? What percentage of our funds has been moved to feed refugees or move families out of harm's way?

It was discovered that one of these twenty-one men was not a follower of Jesus. He was a refugee from the nation of Chad and captured by terrorists. As he knelt there in the sand, watching these Christians give their life for Christ, he was moved. When his turn came to denounce Christ or lose his life, he boldly responded, "Their God is my God!"[23] I am in tears as I think about this. The martyrdom of these believers inspired this unbeliever to follow their example. He chose to give his life for the cause of Christ. What about us? What has their sacrifice moved us to do? How are we responding to the massacre? We need revival in America again!

Where are the Asaphs who are in anguish over the destruction of the God-ordained family? Today homosexuals fight harder for marriage than the church does. In 2015, when the Supreme Court handed down a landmark 5-4 decision making same-sex marriage constitutional, the church expressed outrage for a few days. Then she fell back into her slumber. The ruling was heralded by gay-rights activists as a great defeat for the church as social media posts such as #LoveWins and #GodLoses were shared across the land.[24]

The church didn't lose that day, nor did love win. If anything, the church lost the argument for traditional marriage long ago when we stopped fighting for our own marriages. Dysfunctional families, skyrocketing divorce rates, and numerous pastoral affairs showed the world that the modern church had little regard for marriage. How can you claim the moral high ground when you fail to uphold moral principles in your own home? The church fought hard to keep marriage between one man and one women but failed to fight for their own. When so little value is placed on marriage, how can we expect the world to believe us when we speak of how precious marriage is? We need revival in America again!

Where are the Asaphs who will stand boldly before God and stake their reputations upon His Word? Today many pastors have begun to moderate their messages. They willingly choose to ignore controversially biblical truth in exchange for influence in their communities. Some have gone so far as to call for the church to change our views on what the Scriptures actually say. They say we need a more culturally relevant Christianity. One such author stated, "The church will continue to be even more irrelevant when it quotes letters from 2,000 years ago as their best defense."[25] These leaders rationalize that Scripture must be understood and interpreted through the lens of the culture. How dare we defy God in such a way! We need revival in America again!

Friend, I'm not writing to tell you how bad things are. I'm writing to call the church to take responsibility for how bad we've allowed things to get. It is time for men and women who, like Asaph, become gripped with the reality of what is taking place and fall upon their faces before the Lord and cry out for revival. Let the holy remnant look upon the tragic condition of our land and begin to lose sleep over its current state of rebellion.

God has not forsaken the nation; the nation has forsaken Him. It's time we as the church begin to take responsibility for how bad we have allowed things to get! If times are desperate, if the heavens are shut up and there is no rain, it means God's people have lost their way. But there is hope!

I WILL REMEMBER THE WONDERS OF THE LORD!

Asaph's affliction brought him to the place where he began to encourage himself by looking back and remembering the past moves of God. He recalled how God had delivered His people from the mighty Egyptians. Nothing could have seemed bleaker than four hundred years of slavery under a pharaoh who ruled with an iron fist. Pharaoh had slaughtered children and treated God's people like dogs. It was a desperate time, but God saw their distress and answered powerfully, just as Aspah wrote:

> The waters saw You, O God; the waters saw You, they were afraid; the depths also trembled. The clouds poured out water; the skies sent out a sound; Your arrows also flashed about. The voice of Your thunder was in the whirlwind; the lightnings lit up the world; the earth trembled and shook. Your way was in the sea, Your path in the great waters, and Your footsteps were not known. You led Your people like a flock by the hand of Moses and Aaron.
>
> —PSALM 77:16–20, NKJV

We too can look back at what God has done—not just in biblical history, but in our own nation's history as well. The stories of previous moves of God invite the sparks of those revivals to reignite something within us. It is not about living in the past but learning from the past, remembering that we've been here before and the answer is still the same.

You can do it personally as well. Look back to the times when God moved on your behalf. Don't live so present-minded that you forget all that God has done for you. Go back to the day you were saved. Go back to when you were healed. Go back to the moment of breakthrough and start to praise Him.

No matter how dark it may seem, if God did it before, He can do it again. He has not forsaken us! The same God who moved in the past stands ready to move in the present. Our greatest days are not behind us but ahead of us. Revival has always been God's remedy for an ailing nation. Go ahead and look back and remember the wonders of the Lord. Then look toward heaven and pray with me, "Lord, do it again, like Cane Ridge!"

*Take heed, dear friend; do not think any sin trivial;
remember it will have everlasting consequences.
O, to have [a] heart for perfect holiness—to be
holy as God is holy—pure as Christ is pure—
perfect as our Father in heaven is perfect.
Oh! what a cursed body of sin we bear.*[1]

—Robert Murray McCheyne, 1840

Chapter 3

HOLY FIRE

The Revival in Dundee

*Pursue peace with all men, and the holiness
without which no one will see the Lord.*

—Hebrews 12:14

August 1839, Dundee, Scotland

ROBERT MURRAY MCCHEYNE's health was failing
quickly. He was only twenty-five years old yet suffered like a man three times his age. His condition was
making it increasingly difficult for him to continue his duties
as the pastor of St. Peter's church in Dundee, Scotland. No
one questioned the work ethic of "Holy McCheyne."[2] He
was a driven and disciplined man who loved God and loved
people. However, the pace McCheyne set for his life came
at a price.

His doctor was growing concerned that the minister's
work was taking a fatal toll on his already weakened body.
McCheyne was advised to take a break, rest, and recuperate.
However, Robert Murray McCheyne found rest to be a difficult exercise. McCheyne hoped he might have found a
compromise that worked for both his body and spirit. He
had been invited to accompany a group of ministers on a

missionary expedition to Palestine. There the Church of
Scotland hoped to establish a work among the Jews living
in the ancient Holy Land. McCheyne had a big heart for the
Jewish people, and this trip would be the fulfillment of a
lifelong dream. His doctor hoped that if the pastor wouldn't
rest, at least the Mediterranean climate might be beneficial
for his health.

McCheyne was merely days away from leaving but was
still in search of a minister to watch over his congregation
in his absence. Though McCheyne had been pastor of St.
Peter's for only three years, already he had developed a deep
love for his people. His dedication to his work and standard
of holiness had earned him respect not only in his church
but in the city as well.

McCheyne felt the greatest need of his people was personal holiness. He truly lived an exemplary life of prayer
and devotion to the Lord. It was this devotion that earned
the minister the nickname "Holy McCheyne." Obviously,
such a pastor wouldn't trust just any man to shepherd his
flock. St. Peter's was the church home of more than eleven
hundred members. The church was built as part of the
Church of Scotland's extension program and was situated
in a booming industrial area of Dundee. The stately gray
stone chapel was hard to miss as it sat prominently atop a
hill. Its large clock tower could be seen for miles. The tower
itself extended out from the front of the church, creating a
grand entryway for the members. Though the church and
its pastor had been in the town only a few years, both had
already earned a great reputation within the city.

McCheyne had heard good reports about a minister
named William Burns. He was the twenty-four-year-old
son of a highly respected pastor in the neighboring village
of Kilsyth. Burns had regularly filled in for his father and

shown himself to be a trustworthy minister with a passion for the lost. McCheyne, feeling prompted by the Holy Spirit, wasted no time in writing a letter inviting Burns to come take his pulpit during his absence. McCheyne hoped William Burns might not only keep watch over the church but also perhaps stir the congregation toward revival.

Yes, it was out of necessity that McCheyne wrote, though the hand of God was surely at play as well. McCheyne didn't know it yet, but the answer to this letter would also bring the answer to three years of prayer and an end to over one hundred thirty years of spiritual drought.

When William Burns received McCheyne's letter, he was greatly humbled. McCheyne was known as a "living epistle" and an "able evangelist."[3] Burns felt inadequate to accept such a position, yet to honor the man of God he felt he had no choice.

William Burns himself was not really a pastor but an evangelist and missionary at heart. He hoped soon to travel west into India to carry the gospel to unreached people. This burden for souls had been with him from an early age. His mother had first taken notice of it when her son was eight years of age. She and William were out one afternoon doing some shopping in town. She had become distracted at one point and lost sight of her son. Frantically she began to retrace her steps looking for William. It wasn't long before she discovered him slumped over in an alleyway. The boy was in tears.

"Willie, my boy, what ails you? Are you ill?"

Through tears he replied, "Oh, mother, mother—the thud of these Christless feet on the way to hell breaks my heart!"[4]

This uncommon burden for the lost increased as William grew older. It constantly drove him to his knees in deep intercession. He would spend hours at a time on his face before the Lord in agony over the lost and over the back-slidden condition of the church. Such a man who is much in God is much with God. Burns's ministry carried a divine urgency and intensity. He made quite the impact on sinners and saints alike. In many ways the evangelist William Burns was a perfect complement to Pastor Robert Murray McCheyne. Both carried a heart for lost souls and longed to see true revival take hold of Scotland.

Robert was overjoyed when word came back that Burns had accepted the invitation. McCheyne had done his job as a pastor preparing his people. His constant message of holiness had positioned the people for a move of God. He now hoped that in his absence Burns might ignite a fire. McCheyne quickly penned another note to the minister, saying:

> You are given in answer to prayer, and these gifts are, I believe, always without exception blessed. I hope you may be a thousand times more blessed among them than ever I was. Perhaps there are many souls that would never have been saved under my ministry, who may be touched under yours; and God has taken this method of bringing you into my place.[5]

William Burns was in the pulpit of St. Peter's the following Sunday. In the weeks following, Burns would move back and forth between Kilsyth and Dundee ministering between two separate churches. Though tiring, the outcome was certainly blessed as both cities were about to be ushered into a great move of God that would change the course of Scotland.

It was late July and Burns was preaching a Sunday morning service in Kilsyth. As he ministered, he became keenly aware of the sleeping saints and lost sinners in attendance. He felt an intense burning within himself to take hold of them with his words. He preached a powerful message on the judgment of the Lord, reminding the congregation, "No cross, no crown."[6] As he spoke, the audience couldn't help but take note of the urgency in the preacher's voice. He aroused them from their slumber and brought them to attention. His words provoked everyone to the point their feelings became too strong to contain. One by one they began to break out in weeping and wailing over their own backslidden condition. The church was suddenly and completely filled with the sound of groaning and weeping interspersed with occasional shouts of joy and praise.

It seemed as if all in attendance that day had become suddenly and painfully aware of the grave danger that awaited them on the Day of Judgment. They now sought relief. It was a supernatural move. Strong, hardened, and mature men began to fall to the ground as though they were dead. They were taken right off their feet and left lying on the floor of the church. Some lay silent; others screamed out in agony.[7]

The power of the Holy Spirit was felt so strongly at the service that no one wished to leave. It lasted until three in the afternoon. That night the evening service continued on the same course. Services were added each night, and the crowd grew each day. William Burns would have stayed, but he had to be back in Dundee for the midweek prayer service.

Burns brought the revival fire from Kilsyth with him to St. Peter's. He shared the testimony of how revival had broken out in Kilsyth and had taken hold of his father's town. At the end of the service he invited all who wished to earnestly seek a visitation of the Holy Spirit to stay and pray. A little over one hundred people responded to the call and stayed. As the extended prayer service continued into the night, the Spirit of God began to break out in such a powerful way that prayer meetings had to be arranged for every evening following. Each night the number of people in attendance grew. When Friday came, there was no longer any room in the church for another person.

The word was circulated far and wide that the skies above Scotland were no longer brass and that the Spirit of God was moving in power once again.[8] That Sunday it seemed as if most of the population of Dundee was in attendance. William preached a powerful message that morning. At the conclusion of his address the power of God descended all at once. It seemed as if a pent-up flood of tears broke forth in just one moment. The entire church was either weeping or thrown to the floor.

Services continued in Dundee every night for months, lasting into the late hours of the night. To make room for the crowds, Burns tried moving the service outside into the meadows, but the local authorities objected, so they moved to the graveyard outside St. Peter's. There a field for the dead was transformed into a birthplace for the sinner.[9]

The effect on Dundee and the surrounding regions was unprecedented. It seemed as if all of Scotland was being affected. The fear of God had taken hold of the country, and the people were convicted toward holiness. Word about the revival was printed and distributed in newspapers that were circulated throughout Europe.

This was how McCheyne first heard about the revival. He was surprised to read about it in a paper he picked up in Germany. He couldn't have been more overjoyed. It appeared that in his absence the Lord had brought the answer to his prayers. He remembered the letter he had written to William Burns just before leaving for Palestine. In it he had said, "Perhaps there are many souls that would never have been saved under my ministry, who may be touched under yours."[10]

The thought excited McCheyne so much that he penned a hopeful letter to send ahead of his arrival: "We have heard something of a reviving work at Kilsyth. We saw it noticed in one of the newspapers. I also saw the name of Dundee associated with it; so that I earnestly hope good has been doing in our Church, and the dew from on high watering our parishes, and that the flocks whose pastors have been wandering may also have shared in the blessing."[11]

McCheyne was back in his church in November. What he discovered was a very different congregation from the one he had left. The reports he had read were certainly not exaggerated. His first service at St. Peter's was an evening prayer meeting. This was a fitting way for the pastor to enter into the revival. He was able to participate in the revival in the same manner it had begun. That night McCheyne found such a crowd that every empty space was filled with people seeking the face of God. They were even crowded on the steps of the altar. The whole of the congregation and even the community was now alive and awake. McCheyne had never seen his people respond to God in such a way. They prayed like people who truly believed God was present in their midst.

McCheyne had found an evangelist who was able to work the fields he had so diligently prepared. Burns's stay in Dundee was short. He soon left for the mission fields of India and China. McCheyne was left to keep the fires of revival burning. He traveled across the region bringing the fires of revival to churches, open fields, and city squares. Thousands responded to the call for salvation, and Scotland was saved.

WITHOUT HOLINESS, NO ONE SEES THE LORD

McCheyne was like a burning ember from God's altar setting his nation ablaze with holy fire. This was a remarkable feat, especially when you consider the fact that he died at the young age of thirty after having been in public ministry for only seven years.

The evangelist D. L. Moody is famously quoted as saying, "The world has yet to see what God can do with a man fully consecrated to him."[12] Perhaps McCheyne offers a glimpse into the divine possibilities of such a man or woman. Oh, to have such passion!

One hundred seventy years after his death McCheyne still speaks to all who long for more of the Lord. Even Steve Hill, the evangelist of the Brownsville Revival, considered McCheyne his favorite revivalist from history. He wrote, "In his short life, Scottish pastor R. M. McCheyne was used of God to influence thousands toward holiness. His memoirs, first published in 1844, speak to everyone hungry for personal sanctification in revival. Of the thousands of books in my library, I cherish McCheyne's writings most of all."[13]

McCheyne shook Scotland so thoroughly in less than seven years that more than six thousand people attended his funeral. The nation mourned his loss. That day shops and factories shut down, and sinners wept in the streets as his casket passed by.[14]

McCheyne's message was holiness. He pursued it within his own life and preached it from the pulpit. It was the constant theme of all his writings and letters. During the revival McCheyne wrote to William Burns the following: "I also am deepened in my conviction, that if we are to be instruments in [revival], we must be purified from all filthiness of the flesh and spirit. Oh, cry for personal holiness, constant nearness to God, by the blood of the Lamb... or all success in the ministry will only be to your own everlasting confusion."[15]

Holy McCheyne believed revival must be built upon a

foundation of holiness. This is essential to understand. The writer of Hebrews instructs us to "pursue peace with all men, and the holiness without which no one will see the Lord" (Heb. 12:14). The message of true revival must always be a call away from worldliness and into holiness. If we are to become participators in God's revival, we must also become partakers in His holiness! A revival that is absent of holiness is not revival at all.

Holiness is not a popular word in the world today. Truthfully it never has been. Holiness is contrary to anything and everything that is not of God. Its very presence in a culture is upsetting to the status quo. Holiness shines like an intense light revealing, exposing, and threatening all who wish to remain in the dark. It is unfortunate that true holiness is seldom preached, much less expected from either the preacher or the parishioner. Its very mention has been retired from the vocabulary of the modern church and deemed as the old, rigid religion of our grandparents. It has been defined as a set of rules and a code of conduct that no one can meet. This is a disastrous misunderstanding of holiness.

There was a time when I would have defined holiness this way as well. I was raised in a Pentecostal church in the foothills of the Carolinas. By the world's standards, the rules were strict. Movies had to be G-rated to be watched. (We even walked out of a few of those because of a reference to God made in vain or a demonic character.) Secular music was taboo, as were proms and dances. We were at church more than twice a week. There were always special services and conferences about the end times, the rise of secular humanism, and New Age/occult activity. For me, this created an environment of fear rather than holiness—one I ultimately rebelled against. I don't believe it was ever intentional, just the outcome of my misguided under-standing of what it means to walk in holiness.

HOLINESS DEFINED

Holiness can only be defined as the absolute nature of God. It is the true essence of everything God is! It exists without measure or degree. As such, holiness is much more than the mortal mind of man could ever hope to grasp. It exists outside of us and is unknown to us. Even the word itself is a foreign term to the natural man. Had God not revealed it within Scripture, we wouldn't know it.

Holiness is the pure essence of everything God is and everything that is His. A. W. Tozer describes it like this: "Holy is the way God is. To be holy He does not conform to a standard. He is that standard. He is absolutely holy with an infinite, incomprehensible fullness of purity that is incapable of becoming other than it is. Because He is holy, His attributes are holy; that is, whatever we think of as belonging to God must be thought of as holy."[16]

Our understanding of holiness must begin here, with God Himself. It is impossible to define or know holiness any other way. One glimpse in the direction of God, and suddenly holiness will begin to come in view.

The Prophet Isaiah got such a glimpse of God's holiness in a vision, and it changed everything about him.

> In the year that King Uzziah died I saw the Lord sitting on a throne, high and lifted up, and His train filled the temple. Above it stood the seraphim. Each one had six wings. With two he covered his face, and with two he covered his feet, and with two he flew. One cried to another and said: "Holy, holy, holy, is the LORD of Hosts; the whole earth is full of His glory." The posts of the door moved [or were shaken] at the voice of him

who cried, and the house was filled with smoke. And I
said: "Woe is me! For I am undone."

—ISAIAH 6:1–5

Isaiah's vision of God's holiness came as a sudden and
violent shock to the prophet. He looked up and saw the
Lord in the fullness of His majesty. Oh, what a vision! This
was a life-altering encounter for Isaiah, where his miscon-
ceptions and false ideas of God were suddenly removed by
a revelation of God's reality. This, my friend, is revival!

Isaiah also saw the sera-
phim that encircle the throne
of God and constantly raise
their voices in praise. Their
words express God's nature—

> Holiness is the pure
> essence of everything
> God is and every-
> thing that is His.

holiness. The word *seraphim* itself means "the burning ones."
They have always dwelled in the presence of an almighty
God who is an all-consuming fire and who dwells in unapproachable light (Heb. 12:29; 1 Tim. 6:16). These angels burn
not of themselves but of the very presence of God. They are
a reflection of God's holy fire. It is very much like when
Moses glimpsed God's glory. That encounter caused his face
to shine with such intensity that the Israelites had to hide
their eyes from him (Exod. 34:29–35). That was after just a
short time in God's presence. Imagine how these creatures
that have never left His side must radiate!

They not only burn with God's holiness, but they express
it as well. They cry aloud to one another, "Holy, holy, holy."
How can they not? It is all they have ever seen or known.
They fly around the throne and glimpse the intense fire that
is our God. In the same way our bodies naturally react and
we cry out when we touch fire, when these creatures see His
holiness, they have no choice but to express what they feel
bursting from within: "Holy!"

Then the other looks toward God and answers back, "Holy!" Then the next does the same: "Holy!" They continue to call back and forth to one another, "Holy…Holy…Holy!"

The exclamation of their voices literally shakes the room. It shakes the prophet as well. Here, in the presence of a holy God, Isaiah becomes painfully aware of two things: first, God's holiness, and second, his lack of holiness. That is why he cries out, "Woe is me, for I am undone!" This vision inspired awe within the prophet concerning God and woe concerning himself. Please pay attention to this. Isaiah was not a novice in the things of God. He had served as a priest under a great king. Surely before this encounter he would have claimed knowledge of God. It is plausible that he saw himself as a holy man, but now in the true light of God's holiness, Isaiah was totally and completely undone. Isaiah had no idea just how holy God truly was before that moment.

We too, like Isaiah, must be become undone by the holiness of our God. Until we have a similar moment in God's presence, true holiness will remain foreign to us. As Tozer goes on to say: "God's holiness is not simply the best we know infinitely bettered. We know nothing like the divine holiness. It stands apart, unique, unapproachable, incomprehensible and unattainable. The natural man is blind to it. He may fear God's power and admire His wisdom, but His holiness he cannot even imagine."[17] Until we encounter God's holiness, it is impossible to know holiness.

WHY HOLINESS?

Holiness is the environment of heaven; therefore, if we hope to find a home there, holiness must too find a home in us. God instructs His people, "You shall be holy, for I the LORD your God am holy" (Lev. 19:2). Jesus reaffirmed the command in His Sermon on the Mount (Matt. 5:48). And the Apostle

Peter restates it in his first letter (1 Pet. 1:16). It was spoken by God Himself, reaffirmed by Christ, and written about by the apostles—can it be any clearer? Holiness is a must for God's people. He has made it the necessary moral condition for the well-being of His creation. When true holiness is present, all is healthy and whole. However, when holiness is absent, all becomes inflicted with the disease of sin.

This is a true spiritual conundrum. God requires holiness, yet we are incapable of producing it. Holiness is the divine nature of God; therefore human effort or mental discipline cannot create a single ounce of it. It does not come from within us because we do not possess it. Every man and every woman comes into this world born with a sinful nature. Each individual is void of holiness. It doesn't take long before this unholy nature manifests itself in the forms of selfishness, deceit, and rebellion. Over time we grow more and more accustomed to this sinful state. Compromise becomes comfortable. Until we are brought to a place where we see ourselves as God sees us, we remain complacent in this sickened state.

True revival invites the light of God's holy fire to come into our lives. It comes as a necessary strike to our sinful selves, and in the light of God's perfection, our imperfection is exposed. This is where Isaiah found himself and he cried out, "Woe is me!" It is an uncomfortable yet blessed place to be.

We must come to the realization that we are truly lost and in a sad, sinful state, for without holiness no one will see the Lord (Heb. 12:14). Until we have been fully exposed to the divine light of God's perfect and pure holiness, we remain oblivious to our absolute, total, and utter depravity.

THE DISCIPLINE OF DEVOTION

I mentioned my upbringing and the misguided understanding of holiness I once knew. Looking back, I can see
the problems with our view of holiness, but I couldn't then.
The men and women of God I grew up around had been
radically saved during the Jesus movement. Before Christ,
they were radically lost; then they experienced true revival
and were radically transformed. Their *response* to revival
was a lifestyle of true holiness. For them, holiness was not
the list of dos and don'ts that I knew. They had been so
radically saved that they no longer had an appetite for the
things of the world. They had an encounter with a holy
God, and as a response their lives reflected His holiness.
This is the discipline that comes from devotion.

As I was raised in that same church, their *response* to
revival became my *requirement*. This is an important dis-
tinction to make. Their disciplined lives came out of a true
devotion for the Lord. This is the proper way. However, I
had not yet experienced an encounter with God. For me,
there was no devotion; it was just discipline. All I knew
were the rules, and as such I rebelled against them.

When we make discipline the sole priority, religious
hypocrisy will always be the result. Discipline can never
make one holy. This is the lesson the Pharisees could never
understand. Discipline is incapable of creating devotion!
Thankfully, when I was nineteen years old I had a powerful
encounter with the Lord at the altar of a church. This was
the first time revival ever touched my life. It was my Isaiah
6 moment, if you will.

There at that altar the holiness of God overtook me, and
I became undone. In a single moment I realized how holy
God is and how lost I was. I surrendered fully to Him.

Interestingly after that encounter my *response* to that move of God became a life marked by holiness. In many ways my disciplines looked much like those of the men and women I was raised around. Was it because I was trying to be disciplined? Not at all. The difference was that my disciplined life now flowed from a devoted heart. Everything I did came out of a holy burning passion for God. His holiness had touched me, and as a consequence of that encounter I was changed—set apart, holy unto the Lord!

We must understand two things. First, holiness is a requirement for all who wish to enter into God's kingdom, for without holiness no one will see the Lord! Second, holiness is not something we are capable of creating within ourselves. Holiness is the divine nature of God, and as such it exists outside of us. This is truly a predicament! What are we to do?

McCheyne wrote, "Our soul should be a mirror of Christ; we should reflect every feature; for every grace in Christ there should be a counterpart grace in us."[18] He later said, "For every look at yourself, take ten looks at Christ!"[19]

The answer, my friend, is not found in looking toward yourself but toward God. Personal holiness is the consequence of having been touched by His holiness. It is there that we become partakers of His divine nature.

Isaiah experienced this moment as well, and he cried out, "Woe is me! For I am undone because I am a man of unclean lips, and I dwell in the midst of a people of unclean lips. For my eyes have seen the King, the LORD of Hosts" (Isa. 6:5).

Isaiah's proper response in this uncomfortable moment was to repent. He cried out before the Lord. It is then that the Lord dispatched one of the seraphim from His side to take a live, hot burning coal from the altar of the Lord to touch Isaiah's lips. The seraphim then said, "This has touched your lips, and your iniquity is taken away, and your sin purged" (v. 7).

No doubt it was a painful moment as Isaiah's flesh was touched with God's holy fire. It was here that he became a "[partaker] of His holiness" (Heb. 12:10). What Isaiah was incapable of producing from within himself touched his life in the presence of the Lord. In one moment everything was forever changed.

To become a partaker of His holiness, we must gaze upon God. In full faith and complete humility we must come before the Lord and allow Him to undo our lives, to let the light of His holiness fully expose us. Let us fix our eyes on "Jesus the author and finisher of our faith; who for the joy that was set before him endured the cross, despising the shame, and is set down at the right hand of the throne of God" (Heb. 12:2, KJV). Look to Him and do not look away! The more you see Him, the more you find yourself in Him.

We must seek holiness in the only place holiness exists— God Himself! There and only there will it be found. This is an intense and scary place to be. Standing in the light of God's presence is uncomfortable and will result in our undoing. Yet it is exactly where we must stay, for it is there that we become partakers of His divine nature. Just as Peter writes, "His divine power has given us everything we need for a godly life through our knowledge of him who called us by his own glory and goodness" (2 Pet. 1:3, NIV).

So look to Christ and do not look away. All things needed pertaining to life and godliness have fully been made available to us in Christ. Open the Word of God and ask the Holy Spirit to reveal Christ in every word. Let the Word show you who God is. As He comes into view, you will realize how holy He is. Then you will become painfully aware of where you fail. In that moment don't take your eyes off Christ. It is there, when we look to Him and find ourselves in Him, that we become a partaker of His divine nature and escape the corruption of the world. It is by Him, and only in Him, that we can find holiness. Invite His holy fire into your life to not only expose you but also to touch and transform you.

May not a single moment of my life be spent outside the light, love, and joy of God's presence. And not a moment without the entire surrender of myself as a vessel for Him to fill full of His Spirit and His love.[1]

—Andrew Murray, 1897

Chapter 4

THE SOUND OF REVIVAL

The Cape Revival

If My people, who are called by My name, will humble themselves and pray, and seek My face…

—2 Chronicles 7:14

1860, The Cape Colony, South Africa

R EPORTS OF THE Second Great Awakening in America had found its way across the Atlantic to the southern tip of Africa. It couldn't have come at a better time. The Cape Colony (now the Western Cape on South Africa's Atlantic Coast) was a spiritual wasteland in desperate need of a similar move of God. This was how the Dutch East India Company had left it. For over a hundred years they had been responsible for not only settling the area but also establishing the churches. Yet in all that time they planted only five congregations, leaving most of the settlers as well as the African people without access to a house of worship. Even worse, they had refused to let any language other than Dutch be spoken within the churches, even though few people understood it. This alienated the people even further from the gospel message. A century of such staunch religious thinking had a toxic effect on the budding society.[2]

Now in 1860, though there were more churches, attendance was poor and prayer meetings were few. The pastors themselves had become discouraged after laboring for years without seeing any real fruit. The stories of awakening stirred up a fresh hunger among the clergy for true revival. As such, a prayer conference was quickly organized to discuss and intercede for an awakening in the Cape. Four hundred ministers, elders, deacons, and church members went to Worcester in April for the conference. Among them was a young minister named Andrew Murray.[3]

Murray had just been appointed the pastor of a long-standing Dutch Reformed church in Worcester. Though he wasn't due at the church until May, he thought it prudent to join the other ministers at the conference to pray for revival. He was glad that he did. In attendance was a gentleman from the United States who offered firsthand reports of the Great Awakening taking place there. He said it began outside the church with three men who started a prayer meeting in New York City. Within weeks that small prayer meeting multiplied until more than fifty thousand people were gathering daily across the city. That prayer movement had ignited a true awakening that swept through the city and the nation. Hundreds of thousands of people had been saved, and the church was revived.[4]

Hearing the reports from America emboldened Murray, who felt called of God for such a time as this. Ever since he was a young boy, he had watched his father spend every Friday in prayer, interceding for revival in the Cape. Though his dad had not yet seen it, Murray was convinced that he would.[5]

Faith certainly comes by hearing! The testimony of the revival in the United States stirred Murray to pray more diligently for such a move in Africa. He knew God to be no respecter of persons, so how could He not extend such a blessing in South Africa? During the conference Murray was asked to lead the congregation in prayer. Murray prayed with such passion that the people were greatly shaken. You could say revival was sparked at that very moment.[6]

Murray's first service in the pulpit at his church was on Pentecost Sunday. This was not a coincidence. He planned it this way to set the tone for his ministry in the city. His prayer was for fresh fire to sweep through the church and the Cape. He spoke that morning on the necessity of a new Pentecost. Murray's preaching was something new for the people of the church. He preached with boldness, clarity, and passion. His words certainly moved them. Murray continued to preach on revival every week for the following months. The preacher knew exactly what he was doing. He diligently began laying the groundwork for revival by creating an atmosphere of expectancy. However, what he didn't know was that the coming revival would be altogether different from anything he expected.

Murray's messages concerning revival and God's heart for the people had a deep effect on a young Dutch woman named Miss Van Blerk. She had spent a great deal of time at a farm belonging to her uncle David Naudé. There she came to know many of the Africans who worked the fields. They seemed to Miss Van Blerk to be hard-hearted, crude, and often profane. When they weren't working with their hands, they seemed to be reaching for a drink.[7] The young lady became burdened for their souls and convinced that the revival her pastor preached about must come not only to her town but to the African people as well.

Van Blerk was rare in her passion, as the majority of the Dutch colonists were prejudiced toward the Africans. They

saw themselves as God's chosen and blessed people and the
Africans as heathens to be conquered and employed into
physical labor, not to be converted. Few showed any concern for the spiritual well-being of these people.[8]

Miss Van Blerk found two others who shared her passion. The first was her uncle David's son, Jan. The other was
an old African named Saul Pieterse, whom everyone called
Saul the Prophet.[9] These three prayed together continually
for months. During this time they didn't witness a single
conversion. However, the more they prayed, the greater the
burden they felt. In fact, Miss Van Blerk became so burdened that she prayed nonstop for an entire week. It was
as if she could sense that something was at hand, and like
a woman pushing through pains of birth, she prevailed in
prayer until the breakthrough came.[10]

The breakthrough came suddenly and violently. The first
outpouring took place one evening early in September in
the old schoolhouse that sat in the center of her uncle's
farm. Several farmhands and Africans gathered that night
for a chapel service Van Blerk hosted. What followed was
absolute pandemonium. The Spirit of God descended upon
the meeting and great conviction struck the room. Africans
were a deeply emotional people, and in the meeting that
emotion poured out in a steady torrential flood. They cried
aloud for mercy and pleaded with the Lord with a deep
anguish of the soul. The scene took Miss Van Blerk by surprise. It came so suddenly that she ran from the room to
find help in leading people to Jesus. The week of prayer and
the outpouring that night took such a toll on her she had to
leave for a week to recuperate back in town.

When she returned to the farm the following week, she
was greeted with a completely different atmosphere. Instead
of the sounds of cursing, the sound of singing filled the air.

Everyone on the farm had been gloriously converted! Her prayer meeting had grown as well. Now everyone on the farm came together each evening for prayer. News began to spread to neighboring farms about the powerful prayer meetings taking place. Each night more and more people came, often staying through the night and into the early morning hours.

Miss Van Blerk sent word to her pastor to come see what was taking place. However, when Reverend Murray arrived, he was displeased with what he saw. This was very different from any revival he had witnessed in the past. The raw display of emotion and loud groanings concerned him. He warned the people to control themselves and sought to bring the prayer meeting to order. Old Saul the Prophet approached the pastor to challenge him. He said, "Try now to throw a dam wall around if you can."[11] Murray was offended and left the meeting at once. He contended that God could not be the orchestrator of such disorder. It wasn't long before the fire that fell on the farmhouse found its way to Murray's church. It too came suddenly on a Sunday evening in a meeting with the young people of the church. That night J. C. deVries was leading a service with about sixty youth. They met in a schoolhouse close to the church. Most in attendance that night were Dutch. There was nothing unusual about the gathering at first. That all changed when a fifteen-year-old African girl who was seated in the back of the room asked if she could pray.[12]

At first deVries hesitated. He wondered how the others would react. Thankfully he chose to let the girl speak. She stood to her feet, shared a verse, and then started to pray in the most beautiful tone and with so much passion that everyone in the hall was immediately moved. As she prayed,

J. C. deVries turned his head toward an open window. He was convinced he heard something unusual outside. It was distant and faint at first, but he was certain he heard it. It sounded like a roar. As he listened closely, the sound itself grew louder and louder like thunder rolling toward him. It came like a violent wind and filled the very room in which they gathered. It was deafening. The effect on the meeting was instantaneous. Every young man and woman began to fall upon their faces before the Lord. They cried out with groaning, weeping, and wailing. It was very much like what had been taking place on the farm.[13]

J. C. deVries might have been inclined to follow his pastor's lead and call the meeting to order, but he was overtaken himself. Never had he experienced anything like this. It seemed as if something powerful and indescribable had taken possession of him. He couldn't stand; he could only kneel and call upon the name of the Lord.

As the meeting with the young people was getting out of hand, Reverend Murray was wrapping up his service in the main hall of the church. An elder came to the pastor to inform him of the chaos taking place in the school hall where the young people were gathered. It became apparent the same pandemonium from the farm had now come to the church.

Murray came at once. He immediately found deVries at the front of the room and asked him what had happened. DeVries tried his best to recount exactly what had taken place but was at a loss for words.

"People, silence!" Murray cried out as he walked down the middle aisle between the young people. But the praying continued. Even deVries had returned to his knees and began praying, feeling he could not stand in such an atmosphere.[14]

"People, I am your minister sent from God. Silence!" Murray said.[15] But there was no stopping the noise. No one could hear him over the sound of prayer. Once again Murray returned to the youth leader and asked him to lead the hall in a hymn.

DeVries obliged and began to sing a familiar song in Dutch: *"Help de ziel die raadloos schreit"* (Aid the soul that helpless cries). No one heard him; the prayers and the cries for mercy continued to overtake the hall.[16] Frustrated, Reverend Murray threw up his hands and left the room shouting, "God is a God of order, and here everything is confusion!"[17]

Had the outburst been limited to one evening of emotionalism, Reverend Murray may have been able to discount this moving of the Spirit. However, it didn't stop that night. Prayer meetings began to spring up around the church. More and more people came into town each night to pray and seek the face of Lord. Revival was taking hold whether the minister wanted it to or not.

Murray couldn't deny the increased spiritual hunger and holy living that came as a result of the meetings on the farm and the evening prayer meetings of the preceding week, though he still was not sold on the method in which God had chosen to visit. His knowledge of revival was limited to what he had seen and studied while at school in Scotland. There he became acquainted with the works of Robert Murray McCheyne and experienced the lasting effects of his ministry. These revivals were marked with a solemn awe and reverent fear. They centered upon the preaching of the Word and the radical conversion of sinners. However, the "revival" he was witnessing in Worcester was very different from anything he had experienced or read about before.

Murray may have wondered, "What if the same epidemic of emotional outburst that has taken hold of the village overtakes the service this weekend?" What would he do if he could not call the meeting to order?

The first service of the weekend took place on Saturday night. To say that Andrew Murray was anxious when he arrived at the church hall would be an understatement. The events of the past week had already stretched this preacher's understanding of revival to uncomfortable extremes. Many pastors might spend years positioning their churches for revival, yet to no avail. Murray had been in the pulpit for only five months, and already the congregation was on the verge of experiencing an unprecedented outpouring of God's Spirit. That is, if the preacher would allow it.

"God is a God of order," he told himself over and over again.[18] Yet he couldn't get past the stirring within his spirit that it truly was God who was at work in what seemed to him to be utter confusion. Was this the answer to his prayers? Could it truly be God? These questions were in his mind as he took the pulpit in the main hall of the church.

It was Saturday evening, and as the sun was setting, the congregation entered the old stately whitewashed church with eager expectation. Everything that had happened thus far—the meetings on the farm, the outbreak with the young people, the nightly prayer meetings—seemed to be leading up to this moment.

Reverend Murray began the service in his customary fashion by reading a passage of Scripture and then offering a few thoughts. Typically he would then call for the congregation to offer prayers, but instead Murray paused. He placed both of his hands on the pulpit and looked over the people. He knew opening the floor for prayer would take the meeting out of his hands. If he opened the door to prayer, he wondered what might become of the service.

This was certainly a turn of events. When Murray had first come to Worcester, getting people to pray was near impossible. Pastors had told him calling a prayer meeting was pointless. No one would come. The people just weren't interested in praying. But what a difference God can make in just a few short weeks. One month ago it was true; few people were interested in prayer. Now a newfound passion for prayer had emerged. Murray could not deny the effect the prayer meetings were having on his church. Where before no one wished to pray, now Reverend Murray paused at his pulpit concerned about too much prayer.

Murray decided to open the meeting for prayer. There was a brief pause. The room was silent. Then an elderly gentleman raised his voice to pray in a solemn, respectful tone. That prayer was followed by another.

So far so good.

However, as each prayer was called out from different parts of the congregation, the passion contained within each voice began to grow.

"Lord, won't You pour out Your Holy Spirit?" cried one man.

Another answered, "Yes, Lord, do it."

One more cried out, "Oh, Lord, convert the unconverted!"[19]

As the prayers continued, the pace and volume of the prayers increased until the hall was filled with a chorus of prayer. Most ministers would have been encouraged by a house so quick to pray, but this young pastor was nervous.

J. C. deVries was in the congregation that night, still shaken from the events of that week. He listened as the people began to pray. And then it happened again. That

same sound that he had heard just a week before began to
roar in the distance. Once again it came rushing from afar
straight into the room. The sound filled the hall with such
force that the place seemed to shake. It was as if kerosene
had been poured upon an open flame. The service exploded
into a loud outbreak of prayer. Grown men fell upon their
faces; women bent over with deep groaning. Some fainted
and lay still upon the floor. Everyone was praying in some
fashion—no one was silent.[20]

If Murray had hoped to maintain order within the service, he was failing, as the commotion was impossible to
contain. He helplessly called the meeting to order from the
pulpit, but to no avail. The harder he tried to stop it, the
louder the prayers grew.

With no other course left, he abandoned the pulpit and
began to move about the room from one individual to
the next.

"Stop this at once," he demanded. "God is a God of order.
Quiet yourself!"[21]

No matter what Murray tried, he simply seemed to make
matters worse. A gentleman knelt before him crying aloud
for salvation. The minister knelt down with the man to
console him, but his words brought no relief. He arose at
a complete loss for what to do. That was when he felt a tap
upon his shoulder.

He turned to see a man standing at his side whom he
did not recognize. For the pastor it might as well have been
an angel sent from the Lord, as his presence had a similar
effect. The man looked straight into Murray's eyes and with
a stern compassion offered the minister some encouraging
words that would set this move of God into place: "I think
you are the minister of this congregation: be careful what
you do, for it is the Spirit of God that is at work here. I have

just come from America, and this is precisely what I witnessed there."[22]

Andrew Murray paused to consider the words he just heard. Immediately he remembered the conference that had taken place just five months earlier and the prayer he prayed that shook not only himself but the people as well. He asked that God would send a move of the Spirit similar to the awakening in America.[23] He wondered if this could now be the answer to that prayer. Had God truly come?

If so, this was nothing like what he had imagined. So often when we pray, we envision the answer to our prayers. Andrew Murray was no different. In his immaturity he expected God to move in a similar fashion in Worcester as he had read about in his studies. However, revival is a spark that often falls where the tinder is the driest, igniting a fire that cannot be controlled. He had hoped the church would be the tinder box, but God had other plans. While Murray was focused on the church house, the Lord first found a farm house. It was there the Holy Spirit chose to descend upon an overlooked and forgotten people—the Africans. It was through them that this present fire would take hold of not only the church house but also soon every house.[24]

The stranger said, "Be careful what you do, for it is the Spirit of God that is at work here."[25] The man's words came as a great relief. Murray need only let this fire burn until it took full hold of the people. That night, after weeks of fighting, Andrew Murray fully surrendered, welcoming revival into the church and consequently across the Cape.

THE PRAYER THAT BIRTHS REVIVAL

The fire that came that day in the church would continue to burn for two years across the entirety of the Cape, touching every home. Before revival the Cape was a spiritual wilderness. Afterward it became a spiritual oasis. It was noted that after just a few short months, you would be hard pressed to find a home that had not been touched by revival. The religious apathy that once marked the churches had given way to a renewal. Even the critics and skeptics had to note that the conduct of the inhabitants of the Cape had changed dramatically.

Revival comes as a response. It is heaven's answer to the sustained cries and petitions of God's people. This is the promise God gave Solomon at the dedication of the first temple. He said, "If My people, who are called by My name, will humble themselves and pray, and seek My face and turn from their wicked ways, then I will hear from heaven, and will forgive their sin and will heal their land" (2 Chron. 7:14).

Study the great moves of the past, and you will find that every revival is preceded by the passionate prayers of a people who have firmly made up their minds that revival is the only solution. This was certainly true for the revival that transformed the Cape. It came not only as an answer to a pastor's prayers, but even more as an answer to the cries of a people who refused to take no for an answer. God answered with a sound, and it humbled an entire country in a matter of months, including a pastor who at first didn't recognize the answer to his own prayer.

Prayer creates an atmosphere for revival. The First and Second Great Awakenings came on the heels of prayer. The Welsh Revival started with a group of praying young people.

The Azusa Street Revival came out of a prayer service in a home. The Brownsville Revival came at the end of one and a half years of prayer. Revival comes as a response to prayer. There is no other way—period!

I have often heard it said that if you want to know how popular the church is, come on Sunday morning. If you want to know how popular the pastor is, come on Sunday night (assuming the church still has Sunday night services). If you want to know how popular God is, come to the prayer meeting. That is both telling and true. Sunday morning services primarily speak to the people, but the prayer service speaks to God. With that being the case, is it

> Revival comes as a response. It is heaven's answer to the sustained cries and petitions of God's people.

any wonder revival is absent in the church? The modern church prioritizes speaking to man while minimizing speaking to God.

Leonard Ravenhill wrote, "The Cinderella of the church of today is the prayer meeting."[26] The prayer meeting, if she exists at all, is relegated to a dark corner somewhere in the church on an off night, so there is little expectation that anyone will pay her any attention. She goes about unnoticed, unloved, and uncelebrated, yet she is the one that keeps the house clean. She prepares the food in secret and makes the house ready for the guests. Day after day she kneels in humility and yet goes unappreciated. However, when the true Prince comes, she is the one He is looking for. He searches her out and will raise her up from the cinders and elevate her to the palace.

Ravenhill goes on to say, "No man is greater than his prayer life. The pastor who is not praying is playing; the people who are not praying are straying. The pulpit can be a shop window to display one's talents; the prayer closet allows no showing off. Poverty-stricken as the church is today in many things, she is most stricken here, in the place of prayer. We have many organizers, but few agonizers; many players and payers, few pray-ers; many singers, few clingers; lots of pastors, few wrestlers; many fears, few tears; much fashion, little passion; many interferers, few intercessors; many writers, but few fighters. Failing here, we fail everywhere."[27]

Do you believe that prayer works? Can you testify that you have seen God move as a result of your prayers in the past? Can you connect a breakthrough or a miracle in your life to your own prayers? Do you believe in the power of prayer? I've asked that question to thousands of people, and almost unanimously the answer is always a resounding, "Yes!"

If it is true that you, me, and the church as a whole believe that prayer works, why then do we pray so little? Why is prayer the last place we run to? Why do we wait until everything falls apart before we throw our hands up in the air and cry out to God?

You may offer a thousand excuses. I've echoed them in my life as well. Every day brings a mountain of responsibilities and worries. Yet the person who fails to pray says with his silence, "God, I've got this on my own." Yes, there is so much that we must do each and every day—so much that we can't afford not to pray.

The Lord said, "If My people...will humble themselves" (2 Chron 7:14). Humility is the simple recognition that everything has to be placed in God's hands. Andrew Murray discovered this blessed place of absolute surrender. In order to fully enter into the revival he sought, he had to fully yield to God. It is no wonder that of all the hundreds of books he wrote, *Absolute Surrender* is considered his best.

Such humility is essential for God's people. Humility is often thought of in terms of meekness or even low self-esteem. That is misguided. True humility is having a clear view of both yourself and God. It is coming to the place where you recognize that God is supreme in all things and being completely comfortable with that. Humility is truly being poor in spirit.

Jesus said, "Blessed are the poor in spirit, for theirs is the kingdom of heaven" (Matt. 5:3). This soul poverty is the recognition that within myself I possess nothing from which I can draw. There are no resources within me to meet my need. I am here on earth a simple pauper.

Consider the situations you are currently facing and praying about. If God doesn't come through for you, what is your backup plan? Where do you turn when the answer to your prayers tarry? If it's a financial situation, do you run to your employer or to your credit card? If so, you're not poor in spirit. If it's an illness, is your trust in the Lord or the medical profession? Those who are poor in spirit have no backup plan. They know their only answer is the Lord. There is nowhere else to turn—not because they are poor in this life, but because they recognize that this life has nothing to offer.

This is the place the disciples found with Christ. Peter said to Him, "Lord, to whom shall we go? You have the words of eternal life" (John 6:68). This is the place Peter found himself when he said, "We have left everything to follow you" (Matt. 19:27, NIV). The disciples found true humility, and as a result the kingdom of God was fully available to them.

This is the humility God asks of us when we approach Him. We come into His presence not just out of necessity or even desire. We come to Him because we recognize He is all there is. He is the answer, and there is nowhere else for us to turn. In this place of poverty of spirit we begin to persist in prayer and do not relent until we have taken hold of heaven.

This means true revival is not found in a place; it is found in a position. That position is on your knees in full humility before the Lord in prayer. James writes that "the effectual fervent prayer of a righteous man availeth much" (James 5:16, KJV). If that is true, then we recognize the only answer is heaven's answer, and that answer can only be found in prayer. It is then up to us to fall on our face before the Lord and persist in prayer until the answer comes. That is effective, fervent prayer.

Ravenhill preached that we will live without revival as long as we are content to remain without it.[28] That statement is true. Until revival becomes a necessity, it will never be a reality. As long as we mistakenly believe there is another option, the flesh will continue to seek that option.

Not long ago I was in a meeting with several pastors, and the discussion was about revival. Within minutes it became evident that there was a great deal of disagreement. Some contended that revival was unnecessary and unwelcome. They said it created disorder in the church and was proven to be more trouble than it was worth. Others sought to define it in terms that kept it comfortable, controllable, and containable. My response was simple: "What is the alternative?" Their answer was silence.

Revival requires humble hearts and persistent prayer. The Cape Revival of 1860 makes this very clear. Andrew Murray believed revival would come to the church as a result of his preaching, but it first came to a farm as a result of people praying. There the effectual, fervent prayers of the righteous availed much. Their prayers brought forth a revival that changed a farm, a church, and then a country.

Andrew Murray would later write, "I feel sure that as long as we look on prayer chiefly as the means of maintaining our own Christian life, we shall not know fully what it is meant to be. But when we learn to regard it as the highest part of the work entrusted to us, the root and strength of all other work, we shall see that there is nothing that we so need to study and practice as the art of praying aright."[29]

My friend, it is time to return to a place of prayer! Position yourself before the Lord and invite Him to come visit that position with revival. Ask Him to come and consume everything. Refuse to move until heaven responds with the sound of revival.

When you come back to God for pardon and salvation, come with all you have to lay all at His feet. Come with your body, to offer it as a living sacrifice upon His altar. Come with your soul and all its powers, and yield them in willing consecration to your God and Saviour. Come, bring them all along—everything, body, soul, intellect, imagination, acquirements—all, without reserve. Do you say—Must I bring them all? Yes, all—absolutely ALL.[1]

—Charles Finney, 1876

Chapter 5

BREAK UP YOUR FALLOW GROUND

The Second Great Awakening

*...and turn from their wicked ways, then
I will hear from heaven, and will forgive
their sin and will heal their land.*

—2 Chronicles 7:14

April 1868, Antwerp, New York

CONCERN FOR THE upcoming meetings in Antwerp had made Charles Finney incredibly anxious. When he arrived earlier that day, he found the spiritual soil of the town to be unlike anything he had ever faced. Antwerp was hardened, fallow ground. It was a town so dark that even Finney, the great evangelist of the Second Great Awakening, found himself affected. As he rode through the village, he was gripped by a terror he couldn't easily explain. Here it was springtime, and neighbors should be delighted to be outdoors greeting one another, yet the air around him was filled with the constant sound of profanity. Finney was appalled to see how the people treated one another. The environment was toxic. Nearly every man went about cursing, swearing, and damning one another. Finney felt he had entered a town that resided on the borders of hell itself.[2]

He needed solitude and sought the strength that only comes through prayer. The evangelist quickly retreated to the forest to seek the face of God. He pressed upon the Lord in intercession until the Spirit of the Lord spoke: "Be not afraid, but speak, and hold not thy peace; for I am with thee, and no man shall set on thee to hurt thee. For I have much people in this city."[3] These words came as a great relief to the seventy-five-year-old evangelist.

Finney was able to secure the use of the local schoolhouse and planned to preach there in the morning. This would be the first Sabbath service Antwerp had seen in some time. The town had no church, nor did it have any religious meetings of any kind. The few believers who lived in the town were afraid to assemble because of past persecution from a group of hostile Universalists who lived nearby. The group had run off the last pastor by threatening him and vandalizing his home. Since then, no one was willing to preach there for fear something serious might take place. The old brick meetinghouse in the center of town that once held a Presbyterian congregation now sat vacant. It was boarded up and secured with a lock and chain on the front door. That church sat as a warning to anyone who might seek to resurrect the town spiritually.[4]

He expected a crowd, but he couldn't be certain if the people would welcome the Spirit of God or run the man of God out of town. These were the concerns he had brought to God in prayer. When the Lord finally answered, "Be not afraid, but speak, and hold not thy peace," Finney didn't need to hear anything else. He was now certain that revival would come to Antwerp.

The next morning he arose and made his way to the schoolhouse. He was pleasantly surprised to find it packed to capacity. It seemed his presence in town the day before had at least awakened some curiosity. Charles Finney greeted the people then opened his small pocket Bible to John 3:16. He read aloud, "For God so loved the world, that he gave his only begotten Son, that whosoever believeth in him should not perish, but have everlasting life" (KJV). Then with many tears and many words, he shared how mankind had mistreated so great a love.

Finney was a slim yet towering figure. His face was stern, and his blue eyes were piercing, as if he could look into your very soul. He was balding, but his beard was long, gray, and thick. It surrounded his face like the mane of a wild beast. It was a fitting look for a man whose very presence commanded attention. Speaking to the people with passion and clarity, he exuded great boldness and trusted the Lord to do the work. Not holding back a single word, he began to point out the very men whom he had witnessed the day before.

He called out their sins while letting loose his whole heart upon them: "I told them they seemed 'to howl blasphemy about the streets like hell-hounds;' and it seemed to me that I had arrived 'on the very verge of hell.'"[5]

They could not disagree with the evangelist. He was right. Finney's background as a lawyer showed that day as he began to present his case against the town. Every man and woman in attendance became painfully aware of their guilt before God. Surprisingly no one was offended. Instead they broke into tears. There wasn't a dry eye in the room, including Finney's. Perhaps that was the secret to his success that day. He preached the truth boldly with words, but he displayed compassion clearly with his tears.

This first service exceeded Finney's expectations. It appeared he had found favor in Antwerp. After the meeting a man approached him with the keys to the old brick meetinghouse. He asked the evangelist if he would like to use the building. What a miracle! The very building that first greeted Finney as a warning became a sign of welcome. Revival was coming to Antwerp. Finney graciously accepted and set a second meeting for later that afternoon.

The service that morning had made quite the impact. Those who had been in attendance wasted no time spreading the news. They scattered throughout town rounding up friends, family, and neighbors. The entire town came out that afternoon, once again filling the building to capacity.

As the old evangelist stepped up before the people, he felt something completely new come upon him. He could only describe it as a prophetic unction from the Lord. As Finney preached, it seemed as if his words fell upon the congregation like hailstones from the sky, yet he spoke with love. It was with a divine agony of his heart that he rebuked them. In the whole of his ministry career he had never spoken with such severity, yet no one accused him of being harsh. Again, through much weeping and tears, many were finding the grace of God that always comes upon the broken and contrite.

The revival meetings continued in Antwerp for three weeks. The fallow ground that had greeted the evangelist days earlier was now broken up. Finney preached every day anywhere a crowd could be gathered. Lost souls were coming back to God through genuine repentance.

Finney continued to hold Sabbath services at the old meetinghouse. It was on the third Sunday that Finney noticed an elderly man in service whom he had not seen before. After the service the elder came and pleaded with the evangelist to come to his neighborhood and preach. He said the town was only a few miles away, and, like Antwerp, they had no church. He felt certain he could get the schoolhouse open

for an evening service and gather the town. Finney agreed
to come the following day.

Monday morning came quickly. It was a pleasant and
warm spring day. Finney decided to leave his horse behind
and take full advantage of the beautiful weather by walking
to this nearby town. He figured he would pray and invite
along whomever he might come across on his way to the
meeting. However, the heat of the day and exhaustion from
revival made his journey up the road more difficult than he
had expected. He had to stop several times to rest. He was
afraid he might not make it on time.

Finney arrived late but found the schoolhouse full—so
full that he couldn't enter the building. His only choice was
to position himself within the open door. He welcomed the
people and opened with a hymn. That was a mistake, as no
one seemed to be familiar with the tune. The sound in the
schoolhouse was absolutely awful. Finney couldn't endure
it. He placed both hands over his ears, holding them there
with his full strength. Unfortunately for the evangelist it
wasn't enough to silence the noise. The whole situation was
quite distressful. It wasn't just the song. The town itself was
truly lost. Finney fell upon his knees before the Lord and
began to pray in desperation.[6]

The evangelist had not previously thought about what to
preach that afternoon. He had wanted to see the town first.
Now as he finished praying, he rose to his feet and said the
first verse that came to mind: "Up, get you out of this place;
for the Lord will destroy this city" (Gen. 19:14, kjv).[7]

Finney then began to tell about Abraham, Lot, and a
place called Sodom. He shared how Sodom had become
exceedingly wicked and was filled with abominable prac-
tices. He explained to them that because of the wickedness
of the town, the Lord had determined to destroy the city.

Then he shared how Lot was saved because of Abraham's intercession.

As Finney preached, the crowd became noticeably angry with him. The men began to look at one another as if they were plotting to overtake the preacher. Finney had no idea what it was he could have said that would have offended them so. Their anger continued to grow as he spoke of the sins of Sodom. The situation caused the evangelist to pause, as if he was uncertain of what to do. It was then that he remembered the words the Lord spoke to him just a few weeks earlier: "Be not afraid, but speak, and hold not thy peace; for I am with thee, and no man shall set on thee to hurt thee."

If ever there was a time to heed such words, it was now. The evangelist turned to the people and began to address them directly: "I [understand] that [you have] never had a religious meeting in [this] place; and that therefore I had a right to take it for granted...[you are] an ungodly people."[8] He then pressed that thought upon them with more and more energy. Finney felt like his heart for the people was about to burst.

Suddenly the anger broke and an awful solemnity settled upon the people. The whole congregation began to fall to the floor in every direction with shouts and cries for mercy. It looked like they had been cut from their seats with the swing of a swift sword. They fell at once. Sheer shock fell over the entire gathering. Some were kneeling while others lay prostrate. Some cried aloud while others were unable to speak.

Finney had to stop preaching, as no one was paying attention anymore. He cried out in a loud voice, "You are not in hell yet; and now let me direct you to Christ."[9] He tried to share the gospel with them, but it was pointless. They couldn't hear the preacher. It was a powerfully affecting scene for the evangelist. He had never seen anything like it. His heart was now filled with joy. He wanted to shout and give glory to God.

However, there was still much work to be done. The people had been broken; now they needed to be healed.

Finney surveyed the crowd and noticed the old man who had invited him sitting in the middle of the house. He too was looking around in total amazement. Finney screamed out to him, "Can't you pray?"[10] At that, the man fell upon his knees, and with a thundering voice poured himself out to God. That wasn't the assistance Finney was looking for.

Now the evangelist was alone in his efforts, but he knew what must be done. He turned to the person closest to him. It was a young man who was on his knees. He was crying with the pains of deep remorse. Finney laid his hands on the man's shoulder and put his mouth to his ear. There he preached Jesus and the wonderful work of the cross. As the gospel became clear, the man's pain transitioned to peace. He was gloriously saved! The young man got up and began praying for another person. Finney followed suit, moving from person to person until each man and woman had been brought to the foot of the cross. The service continued for hours until Finney could stay no longer. He left the elder man in charge.

The next day Finney was surprised to receive word asking for his immediate return to the little town. When Finney arrived later that afternoon, he discovered the meeting had not broken up. The people had remained through the night.[11]

As Finney asked about the events of the past twenty-four hours, he discovered the full story of the day before. This little town on the outskirts of Antwerp was called Sodom. There was only one religious man there in the town. That man was the elder gentleman who had invited the evangelist. He was the one who secured the school and invited the community. Everyone in town knew him as Lot. That evening the people were angered because they assumed the evangelist knew this and sought to compare them with the sinful Sodom. As far as Finney was concerned, it was a divine coincidence. Fortunately for the town of Sodom, what fell from heaven that day was not fire and brimstone but the fire of the Holy Ghost.

RADICAL REPENTANCE

Charles Finney, the great evangelist of America's Second Great Awakening, was a master at bringing communities to revival. His most noted revival took place in Rochester, New York, during the height of the Second Great Awaking. It is estimated that more than one hundred thousand people were born again in that revival. The entire city was changed in a matter of months.[12] Oh, how we need such an awakening in our day!

Finney taught that one of the first tasks necessary to foster revival in a community was to break up the fallow ground. He wrote, "It will do no good to preach to you while your hearts are in this hardened, and waste, and fallow state. The farmer might just as well sow his grain on the rock. It will bring forth no fruit. This is the reason why there are so many fruitless professors [ministers] in the church, and why there is so much outside machinery [organization], and so little deep-toned feeling."[13]

I learned a lot about fallow ground growing up on a small fourteen-acre farm in South Carolina that sat in the foothills of the Blue Ridge Mountains. This homestead belonged to my grandfather, who was a master gardener. He knew how to work his fields and produce a harvest. He taught me the value of seed and the importance of good soil. My grandfather would agree with Finney. Don't waste seed on fallow ground. It must first be broken up.

I would see fallow ground at the end of every winter. The

garden had been left untouched after the fall harvest and sat dormant through the winter, enduring the bitter cold and lack of rain. Every day the winter sun beat down upon the ground, baking a thin, brittle crust onto the surface. As a child, I remember trying to walk across that crust without falling through. I might make it a step or two before the ground gave way, making a perfect imprint of my shoe.

Fallow ground is soil that has been left to rest for a season. It naturally hardens over time, becoming resistant to seed. It would be a waste to scatter seed on such soil. Spiritually speaking, this is the condition of so many people both inside and outside the church. Life has been brutal to them. Daily it beats down on them like the harsh sun upon the parched ground. They are trampled underfoot by the situations and circumstances life throws their way. The longer the season lasts, the more hardened they become. Soon they find themselves content and comfortable in a place of compromise. There is little to no conviction of their sinful state. Their hearts are hardened and their ears stopped up. They have become fallow ground, unreceptive to the voice of truth.

A good farmer knows that before he can sow seed, he must first plow the field. He turns the soil over and over again to wake it up and prepare it. Likewise a good evangelist knows he or she must set a plow to the hardened hearts of the fallowed individual to prepare it for the truth. To skip such a vital step would render the truth void in the life of the hearer.

Finney says this is why "so much preaching is wasted, and worse than wasted. It is because the church will not break up their fallow ground. A preacher may wear out his life, and do very little good, while there are so many stony-ground hearers, who have never had their fallow ground broken up. They are only half converted, and their religion is rather a change of opinion than a change of the feeling of their hearts. There is mechanical religion enough, but very little that looks like deep heart-work."[14]

Finney's messages at Antwerp and Sodom may appear harsh. It certainly takes boldness to step foot into a church and call out the sin and sinner by name. Finney came in and laid bare each man's wickedness before the community until he had convinced everyone of their guilt before God. However, he was not being judgmental. Finney didn't come with an axe in hand—he came with a plow. With tears streaming from his eyes, he took that plow to the hearts of the people. He knew his words would inflict temporary pain, but he did so in hopes that those words would ultimately bring eternal relief.

Consider once again the Lord's words to Solomon: "If My people, who are called by My name, will humble themselves and pray, and seek My face and turn from their wicked ways, then I will hear from heaven, and will forgive their sin and will heal their land" (2 Chron. 7:14). Please pay careful attention to the last part of this "if" statement. The Lord says He will "heal their land" after His people "turn from their wicked ways." My friend, in order for there to be a healing of the land, there has to first be a turning of the heart. The fallow ground has to be broken up.

Finney affirms this as well. He said, "When the hearts of the membership of the church are hard and blind and they are in a great measure conformed to this world the preacher sows among thorns. They must be revived. Their hearts must be broken up. They must confess their backsliding. They must repent, have their faith renewed, and put on the Lord Jesus Christ, as a condition of their prevailing either with God or man."[15] There is no other way to see revival: we must come to the place of true brokenness before the Lord. Without repentance, there can be no revival!

I've heard 2 Chronicles 7:14 quoted many times in prayer meetings and gatherings with great attention paid to humbling yourself, praying, and seeking His face, yet little to no emphasis is placed on the call to "turn from their wicked ways." More than once I've heard a minister quote that verse and omit that line altogether. It may have been a simple mistake, but it was a telling one. This part of the verse must not be overlooked.

Why is repentance so seldom preached? Do we mistakenly believe this no longer applies? Have we deceived ourselves, believing there are no wicked ways within us? Do we understand the consequences of unchecked sin in our own lives? Are we casually tolerating sin?

It is time we get radical about repentance!

We live at a time when the word *repentance* has become taboo in many circles. Some churches have gone so far as to forbid its mention from the pulpit, let alone call people toward it. A good friend of mine was interviewing for a position at a large church that boasted a membership in the thousands. He was an evangelist at the time, and repentance was a central message. During the interview the topic of repentance was brought up. The job was his along with a big salary on one condition. He could not preach about or even mention sin or repentance. He was told it was incompatible with the message of the house. How tragic! If you find yourself in such a church, flee like Lot from Sodom and do not look back!

Others have attempted to change the meaning of repentance in an effort to lessen its offense to the flesh. They teach that the New Testament defines repentance simply as "a change in thinking" and that it has nothing to do with "a change in behavior." They argue that any other view of repentance comes from a religious mind-set that seeks to make repentance into a legalistic work. Their claim is that mankind is incapable of turning from his wicked ways (something I agree with).

These slick preachers contend that trying to repent is akin to earning your salvation. They teach that since we are saved by grace and grace alone, repentance is unnecessary. You just need to change your mind about the nature of your sin. Christ paid the full price for all your sins— past, present, and future. Therefore you don't need to do anything. Don't think about your sin. Just accept that all is well. Jesus loves you just as you are. This damnable doctrine of false grace actually cheapens and weakens true grace.

I wonder if these preachers have read Christ's letter to the seven churches in Revelation. To five of the seven churches the Lord is clear: "Repent, and do the works you did at first, or else I will come to you quickly and remove your candlestick from its place, unless you repent" (Rev. 2:5). He doesn't say change your thinking. He says to change your behavior. Contrary to the popular grace message, Jesus *is* concerned about our works. He comes to inspect the tree to see if it is bearing good fruit.

It is true that no one is saved by his works. Paul makes it perfectly clear: "For by grace you have been saved through faith, and this is not of yourselves. It is the gift of God, not of works, so that no one should boast" (Eph. 2:8–9). We are not saved *by* our works, but we are saved *for* good works. Paul continues, "For we are His workmanship, created in Christ Jesus for good works, which God prepared beforehand, so that we should walk in them" (Eph. 2:10).

Please hear me clearly. Grace is both amazing and powerful. Yes, grace allows us to come to God just as we are. However, grace is far too powerful to leave us as we are. It transforms us and changes us. By His grace we are conformed each and every day to become more and more like

Jesus (2 Cor. 3:18). Grace enables us to do what we can't do in our flesh. Grace is God's enabling power to be all that Jesus is, be all Jesus does, and be all Jesus wants. That is grace! If your life looks no different after an encounter with the cross, it's time to question what cross you encountered!

It is true that man left to himself is incapable of genuine repentance. We are unable to turn from our own wicked ways. Thankfully we are not saved by works but by God's grace. It is by grace that God exposes our sin. It is by grace that God enables us to repent of our sins. And it is by grace that God saves us from our sin. Therefore repentance is not a work of the flesh; it is a work of grace. As Paul teaches, "Do you despise the riches of His goodness, tolerance, and patience, not knowing that the goodness of God leads you to repentance?" (Rom. 2:4). If repentance is work, then the working is God's. We need only yield and let His work be complete in us. Each one must make the choice: resist His grace or repent by grace.

This is important because 2 Chronicles 7:14 makes it clear: without repentance, revival is impossible. There has to be a turning of the heart before there is a healing of the land. To remove or redefine repentance guarantees that revival will never touch our lives. The ground must be broken up!

Are you looking for revival to be cultivated in your own heart? Then let the fallow places be broken up. Where do you need the blade of the Lord's plow to pass through your life? Are there any wicked

> If your life looks no different after an encounter with the cross, it's time to question what cross you encountered!

ways in you? What sin still needs to be dealt with? I plead with you, ask the Holy Spirit to conduct a thorough search of your heart. Invite Him to turn over every rock, check every corner, and expose the deep secret places. Pray as David prayed: "Search me, O God, and know my heart; try me, and know my anxieties; and see if there is any wicked way in me, and lead me in the way everlasting" (Ps. 139:23–24, NKJV).

What is a wicked way? A wicked way is anything contrary to the nature of God. Simply put, it is sin. Sin is anything Jesus would not do. If He wouldn't do it, say it, or think it—it is sin. Sin has no place in the life of God's holy people. It must be treated with great seriousness. Just as a mother despises an illness in her child, so must we despise the presence of sin in our lives. There is no such thing as big sin or little sin. All sin is a deadly, toxic disease that separates us from the presence of God.

Finney said, "Sin is the most expensive thing in the universe. Nothing else can cost so much. Pardoned or unpardoned, its cost is infinitely great. Pardoned, the cost falls chiefly on the great atoning substitute; unpardoned, it must fall on the head of the guilty sinner."[16]

Sin has a price, and that cost is far more than you could ever pay. It cost Christ a great deal as every last drop of His blood was spilled on our behalf. Upon the cross Jesus took upon Himself your sins and took the full punishment those sins deserved. It was a great price to pay. Truly we owed a debt we could not pay, and He paid a debt He did not owe. Talk about grace! You and I could never fully appreciate the fullness of the price He had to pay.

In writing about wicked ways, the Apostle Paul states that "the works of the flesh are revealed, which are these: adultery, sexual immorality, impurity, lewdness,idolatry, sorcery, hatred, strife, jealousy, rage, selfishness, dissensions, heresies, envy, murders, drunkenness, carousing, and the like" (Gal. 5:19–21).

Look at that list again. Don't just fly through the words,

but stop on each one and ask the Holy Spirit to show you if there is even a root of such wickedness within you. Are you in adultery? Do you have an adulterous heart? Do you look upon the opposite sex with lust in your heart? How easy is your head turned, and how quickly do you look away? Are you having an affair? Do you have feelings for someone else? Are you getting too close and comfortable with a coworker? My friend, let the Holy Spirit search your heart. Are there any wicked ways within you?

Let Him probe further. Do you entertain yourself with unclean things? Are you grieved when you view filth on the television or in movies? Do you laugh at obscene jokes? Do you feel compelled to turn the channel, or do you watch more intently? What about idolatry? Are there things in your life you've elevated above God? What things would be hard for you to part with? Why? Do you get jealous over the success, positions, or possessions of someone else? Do you talk about others behind their backs? Are you carrying bitterness, unforgiveness, and offense toward someone in your past? Wicked ways are more a part of us than we care to admit!

Paul concludes this list with "and the like." In other words, the apostle makes it clear this list is by no means exhaustive. We must not play the silly games of sinners that say, "If he didn't mention my sin, then all is OK." Finney in his lecture on breaking up the fallow ground invites us to consider even more "wicked ways."[17] I have edited them for the sake of clarity and space and provide them here.

- **Ingratitude:** Do you express gratitude quickly in any and all situations? Are you thankful for what you have? When is the last time you praised God for His many blessings in your life? Do you feel entitled to things?

- **Lack of love for God:** Have you told Him you love Him today? Is Jesus the first thing you think about in the morning and the last thing you think about as you go to bed? Can you honestly say you love the Lord with all your heart, soul, and strength?

- **Neglect of the Bible:** Is your Bible dusty? Have you hidden His Word in your heart? What is your favorite scripture? How quickly does His Word come to your mind?

- **Unbelief:** Do you have faith in God? Do you doubt God's ability to meet your current needs? Do you trust easily? Do you hope for the best in people?

- **Neglect of prayer:** How often do you pray? Do you have a rich prayer life? Did you pray today? Do you need to pray more?

- **Neglect of the means of grace:** Is church attendance important to you? Are you forsaking the assembly of the saints? Are you giving obediently to the Lord? Have you found a place to serve in God's house?

- **Love for others:** Do you show genuine love to others? Are you looking out for others? Do you care for lost souls? When is the last time you shared the gospel?

- **Neglect of duties:** Are you taking care of your family? Are you serving your employer to the very best of your ability? Are you caring for your own health? Are you maintaining a healthy weight?

- **Self-control:** Do you have the ability to tell
  yourself no? Are there habits, addictions, and
  mentalities you find hard to break?

Going through this list is a sobering exercise. I see where I still fall short and need to repent before the Lord. A man or woman without God is utterly and totally lost. The song is true, "Amazing grace, how sweet the sound that saved a wretch like me."[18] I am thankful He saved this wretch! At this moment I am even more convinced of just how completely dependent I am upon His grace.

Finney encourages each person to "take all these questions solemnly upon their knees before God, and there, in the light of the great law of Christ, settle these questions as in view of the solemn judgment. Let them push these questions to a thorough repentance and breaking down before God. Let them not stop short of a thorough sense of forgiveness and reconciliation with God."[19]

Want revival? Then it's time to get radical about repentance! Break up that fallow ground. Let the Holy Spirit thoroughly examine your life. Don't be offended. Invite the plow of His Word to open you up. Let Him make you uncomfortable. Look in the mirror of Christ until you are truly broken before Him, and then let His grace enable true repentance, for without repentance revival is impossible.

Lord Jesus, help us now through the Holy Spirit to come face to face with the cross....Put us all under the Blood....We thank thee for the blood....O open the heavens. Descend upon us now. Tear open our hearts—tear—give us such sight of Calvary that our hearts may be broken....Open our hearts to receive the heart that bled for us....Do what thou wilt with us. If we are to be fools—make us fools for Thee. Take us, spirit, soul and body. We are Thine....Forbid that we should think what men say of us.[1]

—Evan Roberts, 1906

Chapter 6

"LORD, BEND US!"

The Welsh Revival

*Your kingdom come; Your will be done
on earth, as it is in heaven.*

—Matthew 6:10

October, 31 1904, Loughor, Wales

EVAN ROBERTS WAS a passionate twenty-seven-year-old from the mining town of Loughor. He had a quiet demeanor yet displayed a deep desire for the things God. This tall, slim Welshman with fair skin and dark, wavy hair was rarely seen without a Bible in hand.[2] His devotion to God was so intense that by the time he was twenty, he was considered by many to be a true fanatic.[3] Roberts, however, was unmoved by the impressions of men; he instead desired the attention of heaven. He had an inescapable pull deep within his being to be fully surrendered to Christ.

It was early fall in Wales, and the air was growing colder with each passing day. Already the autumn leaves were beginning to change, putting on their annual display of bright colors. Roberts had just enrolled himself into a grammar school in Newcastle. He was hoping to go into full-time ministry but needed to obtain a basic education before entering seminary. Roberts came from a coal-mining family. They were devout, religious people who taught their boy discipline yet failed to give him a proper education. He had only been in Newcastle a few months but was already finding the time away from home to be beneficial for both his studies and his spirituality.[4]

His hunger for the Lord continued to grow. When he wasn't studying or praying, he was attending services at local churches. He was convinced that a massive revival was imminent, and he refused to miss it. When Roberts heard that evangelist Seth Joshua would be speaking at a nearby conference, he made sure to attend. Joshua had long prayed that God might raise up a young man from the coal mines to shake all of Wales.[5] Little did he know that God was about to answer his prayer.

The first service took place Wednesday, September 28, 1904.[6] Roberts arrived that night with great expectation. He had just recovered from a severe cold and was cautioned against going, but nothing could keep him away. That first night Roberts made up his mind to fully surrender to Christ.[7] The following morning Roberts attended an early morning chapel service. It lasted only an hour, and little was remarkable about the meeting. As Joshua was closing the service, he prayed a prayer that caught Evan Roberts's attention. He said, "O Lord, bend us."[8] Though Joshua didn't emphasize the words, they resonated with Roberts and seemed to erupt within his own spirit. At once he heard the spirit of God say, "That is what you stand in need of."[9]

For more than thirteen years Roberts's deepest desire was to be filled with the Holy Spirit. He had heard about it and read about it, but he was not certain how to obtain such a blessing. He now felt certain that God was offering the baptism at this moment. His heart began to overflow, and his faith began to rise. When the second service began later that day, Roberts felt he was about to burst. The service was opened for public prayer, and one by one different individuals began to stand and pray aloud. As they prayed, Roberts felt an unexplainable supernatural energy enter his body. It took him by force. He held his breath and began to tremble, shaking down to his knees. This powerful force began to increase more and more within him until finally it burst forth from him.[10]

"For God commendeth His love!"[11] He shouted it from the depths of his soul, then fell to his knees and stretched out his arms on the pew in front of him. Sweat began to pour down his face, and tears flowed from his eyes as he cried, "Bend me, bend me, bend me, Oh! Oh! Oh! Oh! Oh!"[12] The experience lasted several minutes and was at times too much for him to bear. It was there that Roberts was endued with power from on high.

Life was very different after this encounter with the Spirit of God. Roberts felt renewed strength in his body and great boldness to preach. He had always been somewhat timid, but now he had no fear toward any man. He found that praise was always on his lips, and an intense burden for the lost now gripped his heart. Visions and dreams from the Lord became a common occurrence. In one he saw all of Wales lifted up to heaven. The Spirit of God descended upon the land bringing the greatest revival Wales had ever known. Roberts was certain that revival was now at hand, and soon one hundred thousand souls would be saved.[13]

It was Monday, October 31, when Evan Roberts awoke feeling compelled to return at once to his hometown. He wasted no time and caught the first train back to Loughor. His family was surprised to see him—even more so when they heard the reason for his sudden arrival. He said he was to preach to the youth that evening in their home church. Roberts's mother was caught off guard, as she was unaware of a service scheduled for that night.[14]

Her son had not yet asked the pastor, but he was certain. "You shall see there will be a great change at Loughor in less than [two weeks]," he said. "We are going to have the greatest revival that Wales has ever seen."[15]

His family wasn't sure what to think of him. Had he lost his mind, or was something great about to happen? Roberts's brother Dan was at home that afternoon. He had been unable to return to work as his eyesight was beginning to deteriorate. He was told that he would likely lose his vision completely. When he shared this with his brother, Roberts called Dan over and said, "Your eyes will recover alright suddenly. The Lord needs you." Immediately his sight returned.[16]

Roberts left for Moriah Chapel to ask his pastor about preaching a revival service for the young people in the church. The pastor, Daniel Jones, agreed that Roberts could conduct the meeting directly following the evening service.[17] That night Pastor Jones announced the special meeting for the young people would take place afterward in the chapel adjacent to main auditorium.

Seventeen people gathered for Roberts's first revival service, four of whom were from his own family.[18] They met in Moriah's old sanctuary. It still looked very much like a church, though smaller than the new auditorium. The seating was divided into three sections on the main floor, each with six rows of long wooden pews. Each section sat at a slight angle, and the pews fanned out around the small pulpit area up front. The room also had a balcony that provided another three rows above each section. The room felt massive for seventeen people. Roberts, however, was not deterred. He had heard from God.

Roberts opened the meeting by explaining why he had come and how he believed many young people were about to be saved in Loughor. He shared the vision he had of Wales being lifted to heaven and urged those gathered to prepare themselves for the baptism of the Holy Spirit.

He said, "Now, this is the plan I have taken under the guidance of the Holy Spirit—There are four things to be right: (1) If there is some sin or sins in the past not confessed, we cannot have the Spirit. Therefore, we must search, and ask the Spirit to search us. (2) If there is something doubtful in our life, it must be removed—something we say of it we do not know whether it is wrong or right. This thing must be removed. (3) Total surrender to the Spirit. We must do and say all He asks us. (4) Public confession of Christ. These are the four things leading us to the grand blessing."[19]

Roberts then invited those present to confess Christ publicly. No one was sure what to do. This was a very different way of conducting a meeting. They were not used to being addressed so directly.[20] As such, they were reluctant to speak at first. Roberts still was undeterred as everyone remained silent in their seats. He continued to speak and then prayed with them for more than two hours until each person present that night stood and confessed Christ before one another.[21]

In the week that followed, Roberts continued to hold services every night. Though few people attended, everybody in town was talking about them. They were divided. No one knew what to think of the young minister and his style. Some questioned Roberts's mental health. Yet there was no denying the effect the meetings were having on the young people of the community. Parents saw an instant change in the behavior of everyone who attended. They were totally different people.[22]

By the week's end a total of sixty-five people had publicly

confessed Christ. So far the revival had only been a small flicker, but it was about to finally catch fire. It was Sunday, and Roberts held yet another revival meeting following the evening service. By this time attendance had grown significantly. The old chapel was packed. It wasn't just young people either. Parents and even members of other congregations came to see the revival for themselves. Some came with eager anticipation, but most came out of curiosity.[23] The church and town still weren't sure about Evan Roberts. That was about to change.

Roberts opened the service in his typical fashion. He invited a young man to read a portion of Scripture aloud. That was followed by a hymn led by an unlikely young lady. It was just that morning this formerly shy and timid girl confessed Christ. Now with much enthusiasm she proudly stood before the congregation waving her white handkerchief through the air while praising God. The hymn and young lady affected the audience deeply.

After the song Roberts spoke for half an hour about the importance of obedience—especially obedience to the Spirit of God. Roberts didn't speak from behind the pulpit. He walked up and down the aisles, addressing the people directly. From time to time he stopped to question those sitting in the pews.[24] He went person to person, asking them if they were willing to stand and confess Christ. That night fifty stood and professed Jesus as Lord. One was a young boy with a speech impediment. Not only did he confess Jesus as his Savior, but he also asked that the church pray for him. "P-p-p-p-p-r-r-r-r-ay-ay f-f-f-o-o-o-o-r-r-r m-m-m-m-me." His request was stirring and affected everyone. The place streamed with tears.[25]

The service came to a close just before midnight. However, Roberts felt now was the time for the Spirit to descend upon the people. He asked those who had confessed Christ to remain and receive the Spirit of God. The majority of people left, but sixty remained.[26]

The doors to the church were locked; Roberts then asked everyone to gather within a circle for prayer. He taught them to pray, "Send the Spirit now, for Jesus Christ's sake."[27] He encouraged them saying, "We must believe that the Spirit will come, not think He will come; not hope He will come, but firmly believe that He will come."[28] He then opened the meeting to each person to sing, pray, or testify. He started with the person closest to him and then invited the next person to follow, until all had an opportunity. The presence of the Lord was felt strongly, and many in the room were visibly shaken. However, Roberts still did not feel that the Spirit had fully come. He encouraged them to pray again, this time adding to the prayer, "Send the Spirit more powerfully, for Jesus Christ's sake."[29]

They prayed and then prayed again. It was on the third time through the circle that a woman suddenly began to break down in tears, calling loudly upon the Lord. Others followed with piercing sighs and much weeping.[30] Two ladies were so overwhelmed by the Spirit of God that they couldn't contain what they felt within themselves. They began shouting hysterically and caused a stir in the room. Those close by gathered around the two women in both terror and amazement. Roberts assured them everything was all right.[31] He cheerfully exclaimed, "That's it!"[32]

It was three in the morning before Roberts returned to his home. He knew revival had finally come, and by the week's end his prophecy that Loughor would experience a great move of God within two weeks was coming to pass.

I SURRENDER ALL!

That following week news about the meeting at Moriah spread throughout the city. The crowds started coming by the hundreds, then thousands. By Friday the meeting had to be moved from the chapel into the main sanctuary. It wasn't long before both buildings were so full that no room was left for another soul. That same week local newspapers began to report on the move of God. One newspaper from Cardiff wrote:

> A remarkable religious revival is now taking place in Loughor. For some days a young man named Evan Roberts, a native of Loughor...has been causing great surprise...at Moriah Chapel, that place of worship having been besieged by dense crowds of people unable to obtain admission. Such excitement has prevailed that the road on which the chapel is situated has been lined with people from end to end.
>
> Roberts, who speaks in Welsh, opens his discourse by saying he does not know what he (will be led) to say, but that when he is in complete harmony with the Holy Spirit the Holy Spirit (will lead) and he will be simply the medium of His wisdom. The preacher soon after launches out into a fervent and at times impassioned oration. His statements have most stirring effects upon his listeners, many who have disbelieved Christianity for years again returning to the fold of their younger days. One night so great was the enthusiasm invoked by the young revivalist that after a sermon lasting two hours the vast congregation remained praying and singing until half-past two o'clock next morning. Shopkeepers are closing earlier in order to get a place in the chapel, and tin and steel workers throng the place in their working clothes.[33]

The revival's effect on Wales was profound. It was reported that the consumption of alcohol dropped by more than 50 percent. Many local taverns had to shut down for lack of business. Even the crime rates plummeted. There were many days when judges had no cases. Police officers became unemployed because they were no longer needed. By March of 1905 the newspaper reported 85,294 documented public professions for Christ, a number that many consider to be extremely conservative.[34]

Perhaps the most extraordinary testimony came out of the coal mines themselves. Remember, it was the prayer of Seth Joshua that God would raise up a young man from the coal mines. God certainly brought a live hot coal out of those mines and used it to set the miners on fire. It became common for worship services to take place underground during work breaks. The mine shafts were no longer filled with the sounds of cursing, but praise. Even the mules, used to haul carts and drive equipment, noted the transformation. They stopped responding to the miners who no longer kicked and hit them. Before the revival these mules were constantly abused and cursed at. Now they didn't know what to do when treated with respect.[35]

This great revival was sparked by a young man who dared to yield himself completely to the Lord and to pray a radical prayer: "Bend me, O Lord! Bend me!"

Evan Roberts surrendered to the Spirit and was used to not only transform Wales but to stir the world as well. He also taught a nation to surrender. I wonder what would happen if someone prayed so bold a prayer today? "Bend me! O Lord, bend me!"

There is no other position a man or woman might find that is more attractive to the Spirit of God. Already we have discussed the necessity of humility, prayer, and repentance.

Now we come to the position of absolute surrender. Roberts had experienced the blessing of absolute surrender in his own life and, inspired by the Holy Spirit, introduced four simple steps that will help anyone find that place as well. When you consider that God used these four steps to invite revival not only on individuals but also on a nation, it seems it might be beneficial for us to pay close attention.

SURRENDER YOUR SIN

Roberts instructed the people to confess all known sin. He stated, "If there is some sin or sins in the past not confessed, we cannot have the Spirit. Therefore we must search, and ask the Spirit to search us."[36] Such a search brings us to a place of repentance. We've already discussed the importance of repentance. Revival and repentance work together. Without repentance, revival is impossible, and without continued repentance, revival cannot be sustained.

David offers a psalm for the repentant. This man after God's own heart found himself in deep, dark sin. When exposed, David responded by saying: "Have mercy on me, O God, according to Your lovingkindness; according to the abundance of Your compassion, blot out my transgressions. Wash me thoroughly from my iniquity, and cleanse me from my sin" (Ps. 51:1–2). David knew he was incapable of cleansing himself. He could only come clean before the Lord and appeal to God's lovingkindness.

This kind of brokenness and contrition before the Lord is attractive to God. David understood it wasn't his works that appealed to God. It was "a broken spirit, a broken and a contrite heart—these, O God, You will not despise" (Ps. 51:17, NKJV). God will not overlook the broken and contrite heart. He always responds with fresh joy of salvation upon the broken.

Are you looking for revival? Then let the Spirit search out all sin. When exposed, lay it fully bare before the Lord. Become broken before the Lord. The world may say, "If it's broken, throw it away." God says, "Until it's broken, I can't use it." This is why repentance is so important. It brings an end to self-sufficiency and invites true transparency before the Lord.

I truly believe a spirit of repentance is one of the keys to lasting and sustained revival. I was privileged to be a part of the Brownsville Revival. This move of God is widely acknowledged as the longest-running and most-attended revival in American history. It lasted five years, was visited by four million people, and documented more than 150,000 salvations.[37] Many have questioned how and why this revival lasted so long. The answer is simple. The message was a call to holiness and repentance. Each night hundreds of lost sons and daughters flooded the altar and repented before God. It was because of this that the meetings remained pure and powerful.

SURRENDER YOUR LIBERTIES

Evan Roberts went further than the confession of sin. He said, "If there is something doubtful in our life it must be removed."[38] I imagine many will have a problem here. We value our liberties and exercise them to a great degree. I wonder what might be in your life that you'd be unwilling to let go.

Leonard Ravenhill preached a message titled "Pentecost at Any Cost." He asked two burning questions: "Do we want another Reformation in the Biblical style?...Do we really want a Pentecostal visitation of the Spirit that will shatter our status quo spiritually, socially, and economically?"[39]

Consider those questions carefully. Revival is costly and

is never convenient. We bend to it; it does not bend to us.
Those who find revival are willing to let go of everything,
even the seemingly harmless things, in hope of taking hold
of a greater thing. Ravenhill said until we know the answer
to those questions, there is no need to go further. The man
or woman who prays, "Give me revival least I die," has
found this place of surrender.

I have found that a great many people love to talk about
revival. They love to preach about it and even reminisce
about it. Yet for all who seem interested in revival, few are
truly burdened for it. Revival comes at the expense of the
status quo. It shakes up everything we hold dear and
demands we let loose all that is perishable.

> Revival is costly and is never convenient. We bend to it; it does not bend to us.

Consider the familiar story
of the rich young ruler. The
young man came to Jesus and
asked, "Good Teacher, what
good deed shall I do to have
eternal life?" (Matt. 19:16).

Jesus first responded to him as he expected, saying,
"If you want to enter into life, keep the commandments"
(v. 17, NKJV). The man affirmed that he had been diligent
to keep every one of the commandments. Jesus chose not
to challenge the man's assertion, though He certainly
could have. Instead Jesus dove deeper into the man's life
and asked for something greater. He said, "If you want
to be perfect, go, sell what you have and give to the poor,
and you will have treasure in heaven; and come, follow
Me" (v. 21, NKJV).

The man walked away sorrowful because he had tremendous wealth that he was unwilling to part with. When I
read this account, I am struck by just how foolish this rich
ruler was. How could a man of such wealth not be able to

calculate the value of Jesus's offer? Pay close attention. Jesus offered this man a seat at His table. He extended an invitation for this young man to come walk beside Him and the other disciples. You and I understand that the value of such a position is priceless. Jesus didn't even ask the man for payment. He just told him to let go of all the perishable things he called wealth to take hold of eternal wealth. Wasn't that what the man came seeking? Or was he simply the embodiment of Isaiah's prophecy: "These people draw near to Me with their mouth, and honor Me with their lips, but their heart is far from Me. In vain they do worship Me, teaching as doctrines the precepts of men" (Matt. 15:8–9). This rich young man couldn't distinguish between the value of the perishable and the imperishable. He didn't recognize what was eternal and what was temporal. If he had been truly wise, he would not have hesitated to leave his wealth and follow Jesus.

What things are you holding on to that are holding you back? What liberties are you fighting to keep? You may argue that it is a *good* thing. Just because it's good doesn't mean it's God. I imagine the rich young ruler had many good things, yet none of it could compare to the goodness of Christ. My friend, don't let anything rob you of revival. Nothing is worth so great a price! Even if you have the least bit of doubt, why debate? Surrender it before the Lord and go follow Him!

SURRENDER YOUR WILL

Evan Roberts preached "total surrender to the Spirit."[40] He challenged the people to be fully and completely obedient to the will of God. Absolute surrender is a very sobering request, yet it remains a requirement for the true Christ follower.

Roberts experienced a powerful encounter with the Spirit after he prayed, "Bend me!" That prayer is in harmony with the Lord's Prayer. Jesus taught His disciples to pray, "Our Father who is in heaven, hallowed be Your name. Your kingdom come; Your will be done on earth, as it is in heaven" (Matt. 6:9–10). With this prayer Jesus showed the necessity of yielding to the Father's will. If you want to see God's kingdom come, you must invite His will to overtake your will. There is no other way.

Jesus modeled such surrender before mankind. He said, "Truly, truly I say to you, the Son can do nothing of Himself, but what He sees the Father do. For whatever He does, likewise the Son does" (John 5:19). He was fully surrendered to the will of His Father. Jesus did and said only what the Father was doing and saying. He carried this surrender to the point of death.

The night before the cross, we find Jesus greatly distressed in the Garden of Gethsemane. There He wrestled between His will and the Father's will. His flesh fought hard that night, but the Son allowed God to bend Him. That night He truly "made Himself of no reputation, taking the form of a bondservant, and coming in the likeness of men. And being found in appearance as a man, He humbled Himself and became obedient to the point of death, even the death of the cross" (Phil. 2:7–8, NKJV).

One might excuse themselves, mistakenly believing that only Christ could live such a surrendered life. However, Paul makes it clear, "Let this mind be in you all, which was also in Christ Jesus" (v. 5). True revival doesn't come cheap. It requires absolute and total surrender.

We must always remember that Christ is our eternal king. That means He is either Lord of all or He is not Lord at all. Everything belongs to Him. Everything means everything.

Your life, your will, your words, and even your possessions are His. Let Him do with them as He sees fit.

SURRENDER YOUR PRIDE

The last condition Roberts offered for revival was the "public confession of Christ."[41] This was the reason he challenged people to stand and make a declaration in the church. He knew if the people were timid and shied away from putting themselves forward in church, there was no chance they'd stand up in the public square.

Evan wrote a letter to a friend sharing the experience he had when he was baptized in the Spirit. He said that as a result, he had lost the timidity he once had. It was replaced with a holy boldness that allowed him to preach without fear before men. Along with the boldness he noted an intense desire to save souls. Though he had always felt this desire, it now consumed him.[42]

Jesus said, "You shall receive power when the Holy Spirit comes upon you. And you shall be My witnesses in Jerusalem, and in all Judea and Samaria, and to the ends of the earth" (Acts 1:8). I know this may come as a surprise to some, but the purpose of the baptism of the Holy Spirit is not speaking in tongues; it's power. I've met many saints who are content to remain in a church and speak in tongues and prophesy to one another, but when they leave the sanctuary, they are silent in the streets. I have to question what baptism they received.

The Holy Spirit was given so we could be powerful witnesses. True Spirit-filled believers have no excuse for letting a spirit of timidity keep them silent. Absolute surrender means our voice is at the Lord's disposal and ready to be used at a moment's notice. Surrender your pride and confess Christ before men!

ABSOLUTE SURRENDER

The thought of absolute surrender to the Spirit of God is terrifying to the flesh because God rarely calls His people to accomplish small things. He speaks boldly and waits for us to respond in kind. His voice beckons us out of the comfort of a boat to walk upon stormy waters. His will calls us to speak healing to the blind, deaf, and lame. He places us as prophets before stiff-necked religious men armed with stones. He stands us before kings, and we call out their sins. These are just a few examples of the stories we honor in Scripture. These bold believers were bent toward the Lord.

Throughout history faithful men and women have followed in the footsteps of the saints and imitated their lives. These are the Martin Luthers, who refused to recant salvation by faith in Christ alone even though it cost their lives. They are the William Tyndales, who dared to put God's Word in the hands of the common man. Their treachery was rewarded with a stake and fire. We look to the John Wesleys, George Whitefields, and Jonathan Edwardses, who covered the country on horseback with the gospel. These men were barred from churches and removed from esteemed positions because they so yielded to the Lord.

We can't forget the heroines of the faith such as Maria Woodworth-Etter and Aimee Semple McPherson. These women were bold enough to believe God could use a woman as easily as a man. These generals of the faith were used greatly by God because they allowed God to bend them greatly. (We will talk more about women in revival in chapter 11.)

Evan Roberts was a simple coal miner with a basic education. It was easy for people to dismiss such a lowly man.

However, that lowly man yielded himself fully to the Lord. He dared to pray, "Bend me, oh, Lord!" The Lord answered and raised that man up from a coal heap. With such a man, God set a nation ablaze in less than two weeks.

Do you hear that? Do you hear your Savior's call? He says surrender your sin, surrender your liberty, surrender your will, and surrender your pride. He says, "Sell it all down to the bare walls, and come follow Me."

Bend me, O Lord! Bend me!

A man with such a dramatic martyrdom and intense commitment which led to that martyrdom is worthy of becoming a legend.[1]

—Dr. Samuel Hugh Moffett, speaking of Robert Jermain Thomas, missionary to China and Korea

Chapter 7

THE GROUND CRIES OUT

The Pyongyang Revival

Truly, truly I say to you, unless a grain of wheat falls into the ground and dies, it remains alone. But if it dies, it bears much fruit.

—John 12:24

1907, Pyongyang, Korea

PYONGYANG HAD LONG been famous for its wine and women. It was a dark city where sin abounded. But something truly remarkable was at work, threatening to change the city's reputation for the good. Revival fire was sweeping through the city, and Koreans were being saved by the tens of thousands. The revival was so great that one missionary wrote home to report, "The work of the Holy Spirit here would far surpass what we have read about the great revival in Wales."[2] It would seem God wasn't just visiting a nation, but nations! At the turn of a new century a global outpouring was taking place not only in Wales and the United States but in Korea as well. More than fifty thousand Koreans would be saved in Pyongyang in 1907 alone.

Forty years earlier such a move of God would have seemed unthinkable. The nation was closed, and no Westerner dared to enter. It was an offense punishable by death. However, one missionary, Robert Jermain Thomas, was bold enough to believe that one man could bring revival to a nation.

It was the fall of 1866, and Robert Jermain Thomas was standing on the bow of the *General Sherman*. His chest pressed against the railing as he leaned out to get a better view. There it was—the forbidden Korean coastline. He had been patiently waiting for this moment for the past seven days. It had been a year since he had seen it last, and now here he was again. This time he hoped to make it further inland than he did during his previous trip, perhaps as far as the capital city of Pyongyang. He knew it was a mission that could potentially cost him his life, but he was determined. He must bring the gospel to Korea at any cost.

For centuries Korea had been shut off from the rest of the world. By legal decree of the emperor the nation was allowed relations only with China, and contact with westerners was strictly forbidden.[3] This strict isolationism created an obscure society that few outsiders knew anything about. The prospect of penetrating such a place with the gospel was irresistible for a true missionary. Such was the case for Robert Jermain Thomas.

Thomas was a brash twenty-seven-year-old from a small rural town in Wales. He was an adventurer at heart with a burden for the lost. He had spent the last two years stationed in China with the London Missionary Society. He had arrived with his new wife, Carrie. After just three months in Shanghai, Carrie suddenly fell ill and died. That day Robert lost both his wife and unborn child. The personal cost of his missions work had been great. Though his time in China had been rewarding, it was not satisfying enough, not considering the price he had already paid. He was fully determined to do something significant for the Lord. He believed that his strength would best be employed toward unreached lands.[4] That is why the moment he saw an opportunity to board a ship bound for Korea, he didn't hesitate.

The *General Sherman* was an old steam-driven schooner that was under the employment of the British Trading Company. The owners had hoped to make it to Pyongyang and establish trade agreements with the governor. The mission was dangerous, but the potential payout to the investors was great. These matters didn't really concern Thomas. The ship needed a translator, and he needed passage. As the only foreigner in China who had both experience on the shores of Korea and knowledge of the language, Thomas seemed to be the perfect fit.[5]

After seven days of travel the ship entered the bay south of Namp'o, Korea. This bay was the outlet to the Taedong River. The captain hoped to sail straight up the Taedong, all the way to Pyongyang, while stopping at every possible port.

Such a large vessel in the river must have been a strange sight for the Korean people. The *General Sherman* was nearly two hundred feet long. It had two large masts with white sails and a single smokestack. Her noise and size made it impossible to miss, and as such the ship attracted thousands of Koreans to both sides of the river's edge.[6] This was something Thomas took full advantage of. He preached at every stop and distributed Bibles to anyone willing to receive one. He knew the risks involved in distributing such literature, both to himself and to those who took them. If they were caught, they could be fined, imprisoned, or even decapitated. Thomas could only assume that, knowing the personal risk, they wished to read them.[7]

Four days after entering the river, the ship came to a village called Chang Sapo. It was market day, so more people than usual were out. The ship was greeted with scores of curious Koreans. An eleven-year-old boy named Hong was playing in the market when he overheard talk about the foreign vessel in the river. Wasting no time, he quickly ran home and found two friends, Choe and Pai, and persuaded them to come with him. The three boys made their way to the river's edge, where they saw a multitude from their village gathered near the docks.[8]

In the middle of the crowd they noticed a tall man with a pale face and golden hair. They had never seen anyone like him before. He kept shouting at the crowd and handing out books. The stranger's Korean was good, but he used words they didn't understand. He kept saying one word a lot, "Jesus." As interesting as the man was, the boys really wanted to see the ship. Hong saw a canoe sitting close by and convinced the two others to come with him. They rowed out to the starboard side of the *General Sherman* and climbed aboard the boat.

Thomas had just finished addressing the crowd and had returned to the ship for a fresh supply of books. He was the first to notice the three stowaways. He found them to be curious and fun. He took the opportunity to show them around the ship. Before he brought them back on deck, he took them to his quarters and offered them some cakes and gave them all Bibles. As the books were written in Chinese, they could not understand them, but they appreciated the gift from the stranger. He then saw to it they were safely delivered back to the dock.[9]

The boys ran home, excited to share the adventure with their friends. When Pai's grandfather overheard the story, he asked to see the books immediately. Pai's grandfather was a teacher in the village and knew Chinese. His face grew grim when he saw the books. He knew the danger they could bring. He scolded the three boys and told them to throw the books into the river. Pai did exactly as he was told. Hong and Choe were unwilling and chose to hide theirs.

That evening the ship ported for the night outside the village of Sookkai. Nine Catholic Koreans led by a man named Chi came out to the boat bringing a crate of gifts. They mistakenly believed the boat was sent by the French government to rescue them. It had been a year of terror for Catholics in Korea. Nearly ten thousand Catholics had already been executed. The rest were living in fear. Thomas was glad to welcome them aboard, and he invited them to his room for cake as well. Chi was surprised when he heard Thomas speaking Korean.[10]

Thomas had a hard time explaining to the men that he was neither French nor Catholic but a Protestant missionary. They didn't understand the difference. He then assured them that their religious liberty would soon be won, and he prayed with them. He left them several copies of the Scriptures and other religious books.

Thomas felt that this trip up the river had been very successful. Unfortunately that was all about to change. The closer they came to Pyongyang, the less welcoming the villages seemed to be. The crew might have been inclined to abandon the mission and sail back the way they came, but the *General Sherman* came across a sandbar and got stuck.

By the third of September the situation had completely deteriorated. Those on board didn't know it yet, but an order had been sent from the emperor to stop the vessel at all costs and to kill the crew. Hostile forces surrounded the grounded boat from both shores and began to fire flaming arrows upon the ship. Thomas may have been willing to sacrifice his life, but the crew refused to go down without a fight. Using the heavy guns on the ship, they began to defend themselves. The missionary now found himself caught in a situation he had not foreseen nor could he control.[11]

The *General Sherman* had far superior firepower than the Korean forces. However, Korean soldiers used their numbers and ingenuity to their advantage. The commander of the Korean forces ordered small wooden boats to be loaded down with dry brush and set ablaze. The boats were then launched downstream toward the *General Sherman* until the vessel was on fire. After failing to extinguish the flames, the captain gave the order to abandon ship. Thomas remained behind, unwilling to relinquish his mission. He began tossing books from the burning boat toward the shore, yelling, "Jesus! Jesus!"[12]

He stayed as long as he could before jumping overboard with one remaining Bible in hand. He knew there was no chance of escape. Soldiers were waiting for him from every vantage point. Thomas came up out of the water both exhausted and terrified. He fell to his knees before a single soldier, who stood over him with a spear in his hands.

Grasping the soaked Bible with both of his hands, Thomas held it overhead toward the solider and pleaded with the man to take it. It was obvious to the soldier that this man was not like the others from the boat. His actions caused the soldier to pause. It looked for a moment like the young soldier might take the book. That moment didn't last long. The soldier followed his orders and ran Thomas through with his spear before cutting off his head with a sword.[13]

Unsatisfied with only taking the lives of the crew, the soldiers were ordered to retrace the route taken by the *General Sherman*. They made their way downriver from village to village asking about the foreign vessel. They questioned anyone who had come into contact with the missionary and secured as many of his Bibles as possible. When they came to the village of Sookkai, they learned about the nine Catholics who had boarded the vessel. Within hours they arrested all of the men. Chi was identified as the leader of the group and was decapitated.[14]

On September 3, 1866, Robert Jermain Thomas became Korea's first Protestant martyr. He had arrived in hopes of opening the isolated nation up to the gospel. But after eighteen days within its borders, his blood ran downstream, carried out to sea by the same river he had come up while the smoke and ashes from his confiscated Bibles filled the air. To many it would seem this young, brash man from Wales had wasted his life. However, seed is never wasted!

The soldier who killed Robert Jermain Thomas felt grief-stricken the moment after he killed the missionary, knowing in his heart that he had taken the life of a good man. He felt compelled to pick up the same Bible that moments earlier he had refused. He wasn't alone. Several soldiers kept Bibles from Thomas. Some did it out of curiosity; others took them home as trophies. One soldier carried home several, and in an unusual move used the pages as wallpaper for his home. He did it in spite but didn't know that what he meant for evil God would use for good.[15]

For the next two decades the stories would be told about the death of the westerner and his dangerous books. Koreans would speak of the soldiers who took the books as trophies and the one who hung them on his walls. The house itself attracted attention from many who would come to see the walls with the strange markings. Then twenty years after the martyrdom of Thomas the home would come into the possession of a thirty-one-year-old man named Choe.[16]

Choe felt connected to it. He was only eleven when

Robert Thomas had sailed up the river. Though he didn't understand the message the missionary had shared, he was curious who this Jesus was that had the westerner so excited. He also knew there was something special about the book he had been given, so he hid it to keep it safe all those years. When he heard about the home covered with pages of the same book, he had to buy it.

Robert Thomas may have been the first missionary in Korea, but he was not the last. By the end of the 1800s Korea had opened up for a short period in time. Missionaries came in force. In 1891 missionary Samuel Moffett visited Choe after having become acquainted with the story of Robert Jermain Thomas, Choe, and the home with the strange wallpaper. Moffett came to see the house and was able to share the gospel with Choe that day. Choe's journey over the last twenty-five years finally made sense. He gladly received Jesus as his Lord.

Choe would go on to plant the first church in Pyongyang there in his home—the same home that wore on its walls the bloodstained pages of the Bibles Thomas risked his life to bring to Pyongyang. At one time they adorned the walls as a trophy celebrating the death of the missionary. Now they adorned the walls as a memorial to a man who gave his life so that Korea might truly be free.[17]

Over the next fifteen years more churches began to be planted throughout Korea, and the revival Thomas had only dreamed of was at hand. It began in January of 1907. Fifteen hundred missionaries, pastors, and leaders from 150 miles around Pyongyang gathered together for a two-week Bible training course. Throughout the day they were taught the Scripture, and in the evening services were held for any who wished to attend.

During the first meeting 1 Corinthians 12:27 was shared,

and those present were encouraged to get right with one another, "as discord in the church was like sickness in the body."[18]

It was a word the Koreans took to heart. As the week progressed, the Spirit of God began to move powerfully. The revival broke out on a Tuesday evening. The main service had just come to a close. The speaker that night was Samuel Moffett. He dismissed the people, yet few left. A line of men began to form, each feeling an intense desire to confess their sins publicly.

The missionary consented, and one by one each man stepped forward before his peers and bore his soul. The honesty and transparency of these men had quite an effect. Godly conviction descended upon the room. It seemed as if guilty souls found themselves standing in the white light of God's judgment. There they saw themselves not as they thought themselves to be, but as God saw them. Every sin a human being could possibly commit was confessed that night. For Moffett it was incredibly disturbing to witness.[19]

On the platform seated in a place of honor was a highly respected leader in the Korean church. His name was Chu, and it was obvious that he was not comfortable. As each man stood before the audience and confessed, Chu grew more and more agitated. In time he looked to be in absolute agony. He sat there like a man who had just received a death sentence. What no one knew was that he was carrying a great weight of sin and knew he must surrender.

For more than an hour Chu sat there wrestling within himself until finally he gathered up the strength to approach the pulpit. He went and stood next to Moffett. With both hands on the pulpit and his head toward the ground, he began to speak. His tears caused him to choke on his words. At first he was hard to hear, but as he spoke, the words became painfully clear. He confessed to adultery and the misuse of church funds.

Chu didn't speak as if he was addressing the audience. He spoke with a fearful agony and trembled from head to foot. It was as if he sensed that he was standing before a righteous judge who had brought his sin to light. He beat the pulpit over and over with his fist as he cried aloud, "Was there ever such a terrible sinner as I am?" He then fell over to the floor and tossed about in great pain, pleading to the Lord for forgiveness.[20]

As Chu wept and wailed on the platform, the whole assembly followed suit. Some men struggled to stand up. They would rise to their feet, only to fall again. They screamed, tossed about, and jumped up and down like men seeking to free themselves from the chains of sin.

> Sacrifice is the fuel upon which the fires of revival are stoked.

The missionary was unsure what to do. It was impossible to stop. There was no quieting the meeting. He could only sit and pray as the people wept bitterly for hours.[21] This continued until one by one each soul found blessed relief.

The meeting became the ignition point for national revival. This powerful move of God was marked with the same spirit of conviction and radical display of repentance seen the night revival broke out. Over the next four years this fire swept through Korea, and more than one hundred thousand were gloriously saved.[22]

Though It Tarries, Wait for It

Revival came to Korea thanks to the sacrifice of a man who counted his life nothing for the sake of the gospel. At first it might have appeared that Thomas wasted his life. But seed is never wasted. Though Robert Jermain Thomas is not a name well known in the West, many of the nine million Christians in Korea know it. They trace their roots back not to men like Jonathan Edwards, George Whitefield, or John Wesley, but to Thomas and the revival of 1907. That was when the Korean church was birthed.

Jesus said, "Truly, truly I say to you, unless a grain of wheat falls into the ground and dies, it remains alone. But if it dies, it bears much fruit" (John 12:24). Jesus spoke these words signifying His own sacrifice and the fruit that would result when He voluntarily laid His life down. In laying down His life, Jesus demonstrated to all who would follow how true ground-shaking reformation is birthed.

Sacrifice is the fuel upon which the fires of revival are stoked. In order for there to be a true move of God, something must be laid upon the altar. All true Christ followers are urged to "present your bodies as a living sacrifice, holy, and acceptable to God, which is your reasonable service of worship" (Rom. 12:1). That means the only acceptable sacrifice is our very lives. Jesus fully demonstrated that true transformation of a culture doesn't come by the violence of the flesh but by violence *to* the flesh. He sacrificed His flesh and ignited a fire. One seed died, and many more were born.

Paul wrote, "It is my earnest expectation and my hope that I shall be ashamed in nothing, but that with all boldness as always, so now also, Christ will be magnified in my body, whether it be by life or by death" (Phil. 1:20). What a creed to live by—by life or by death! True revivalists, reformers, and revolutionaries understand that dying is the only way to live!

Jesus was the first to lead the way and set the example for every revolutionary who would follow. His very existence represented a radical threat to the world's status quo. As such, the religious and political leaders of His day saw no choice but to extinguish His life in hope of protecting their way of life. However, they failed to realize that in snuffing out the life of one man, they would be igniting a fire that could not be contained. The enemy didn't realize the full power of sacrifice. He never does.

Jesus walked opposite of these worldly systems. Consequently they were violently opposed to Christ, or anti-Christ. They sought to destroy Him so they might remain in power and exalt themselves. As Scripture tells us, "Every spirit that confesses that Jesus Christ has come in the flesh is from God, and every spirit that does not confess that Jesus Christ has come in the flesh is not from God. This is the spirit of the antichrist, which you have heard is coming and is already in the world" (1 John 4:2–3). The antichrist spirit has been at work since the day of Christ to protect its power and eliminate threats.

We see these radical spirits of the Antichrist on the rise in our day. Radical Islam is a vicious one. It says choose Muhammad or choose death. It desires total world dominance, bringing the spheres of power—political, religious, and cultural—under Islamic law. We see it in radical activist groups as well. The biggest in our day is that of the gay rights movement. This antichrist spirit says, "Conform to us or be ostracized in society." Businesses, churches, and individuals have suffered loss because they dared to disagree. This spirit operates on both sides of the political aisle among politicians who love power but don't serve the people. These politicians will lie, cheat, and steal to maintain their positions.

Two nations where the spirit of the Antichrist is clearly at work are North Korea and Iran. These two countries

are among the worst places on earth for Christians to
live. Why? Christianity represents a threat to their status
quo. These dictators protect their power by instilling fear
in their subjects. They isolate them, fill them with pro-
paganda, and censor the truth in an effort to control the
population.

Picture for a moment the familiar images of the mili-
tary parades these evil empires organize. They are state-
ments of power for the world to see. The supreme leader
stands high atop his temple or palace. No one is above
him or beside him. Everyone is kept beneath the leader.
Bright red banners bearing his face adorn the walls in
the capital square. The armies march in the streets below.
Thousands upon thousands parade before him in neatly
lined rows, taking sharp, precise steps. They look toward
their supreme leader as they pass before him in perfect
rank and file. March, march, march they go, all doing
exactly as they are told.

In many ways this can be seen as a picture of the world
today. Multitudes march blindly before the god of this age.
They march in perfect step, one after the next. As long as
everyone complies, falls in line, and keeps marching, everything is fine. However, imagine what would happen if one
man, one solider, decides to fall out of line. As everyone
walks in one direction, one man chooses to defy the status
quo and go the opposite way. Would he not be impossible
to ignore?

Jesus fell out of line, and they said, "Crucify Him!" The
disciples fell out of line as well. They were stoned, beaten,
burned, and boiled to death. Some were impaled on stakes
or hung upon crosses. Others were pulled apart limb by
limb. Hundreds were fed to lions, often with their entire
families, including their children. It was all done before

crowds of bloodthirsty men who found their deaths enter-
taining. This happened because these faithful heroes chose
to fall out of line and upset the status quo. They would not
march, march, march as they were instructed.

Robert Thomas fell out of line. He did what no one else
would do and sailed into the belly of the beast. He wanted
his life to matter, and the Korean soldiers said, "Off with
his head." The antichrist spirit always seeks to eliminate
the threats!

Some may say, "What a waste! What did their sacrifice
produce?" One need not ask such a foolish question. You
just need to look at the people who picked up the bloodstained pages that lay on the river's edge. During the revival
of 1907 a Korean man in his mid-sixties came forward in
one of the meetings to make a public confession. His name
was Chu Won Park (not the same Chu who repented during
the revival meetings led by Samuel Moffett). He went before
the church and confessed that he was the one who had
killed Robert Jermain Thomas.[23]

Forty years earlier this man was offered the gospel, and
he rejected the message and the messenger, but the seed was
sown. That seed tarried over the decades until the season
was right. What looked like failure for Thomas at the
moment of sacrifice became fruit in Chu Won Park in the
season of harvest. The world antichrist system will never
understand the unique power of sacrifice. One man lays
down his life for another, and something remarkable takes
place. What was one becomes many!

Jesus came to the world and said, "If anyone will come
after Me, let him deny himself, and take up his cross daily,
and follow Me" (Luke 9:23). He then did something no
worldly leader would ever do. He led the way. Worldly
leaders ask for sacrifice from their followers first; Jesus

showed that godly leaders first ask sacrifice from themselves! Jesus was the first to pick up a cross. He willingly laid down His life. Jesus came and walked opposite to the world. He fell out of line, and the religious and political antichrist spirits didn't like it.

They thought they took care of Him. They snuffed out His flame, but the fire still spread. Suddenly 120 disciples caught that fire, and then the enemy had a bigger problem. If one man threatened the status quo, what would so many do? Their number grew to thousands in a matter of hours. Once again the antichrist spirit was enraged and sought to stomp out that fire. However, it spread around the world, and now there are billions of Christ followers!

The enemy, the spirit of the antichrist, will always attack what he perceives to be a threat to the status quo. That individual or group will be imprisoned, punished, persecuted, or pressured to comply and conform so they can be controlled. The antichrist spirit says, "How dare you fall out of line and threaten the system we've built!" Today the Christian church in the West faces little to no persecution. I wonder if that is because we have found heaven on earth or because the church is not perceived as a threat.

True revival does not come without cost. Someone always pays a price to bring reformation to the status quo. If reformation is needed, then there will be a man or woman who will pay the price. Nobody writes about people who just walked in the rank and file. We tell the stories of the ordinary individuals like Robert Jermain Thomas who fall out of line and do something extraordinary with their lives, by life or by death. History makers are the revolutionaries who say, "Stop, let's turn around and do this differently!"

Robert Jermain Thomas was an ordinary individual with

an extraordinary cause. All revolutionaries are! He saw an
unreached land that had not heard the gospel. That cause
was enough to inspire him to sacrifice. Revolution is born
in the heart of a revolutionary the moment he or she finds
a cause worthy of sacrifice. Do we not have a cause worthy
of sacrifice?

Our nation is in desperate need of a greater awakening.
This world is in need of a culture-reforming revival. If sacrifice fuels the fires of awakening, then let us offer ourselves
as living sacrifices before the Lord. Fall upon your knees
and contend for awakening in your family, church, or community. Take the ridicule if necessary because you dare to
live differently. Don't buy the lie that one man or woman
cannot make a difference.

The greatest weapon of the enemy is to convince you that
your life is too insignificant to really matter. If he can trick
you into believing that lie, he relegates you to the sidelines
where you will simply become a spectator. My friend, you
were not called to spectate in this next great move of God.
You were called to participate.

As I've studied the stories of revival, I have come across
countless "little people" who fell out of line and made a difference for the rest of the world. The common trait of each
of these individuals is that they chose to die to self to produce life in someone else. In the end all of us give our life
for something. We come into the world, and one thing is
apparent: each of us was born to die. The moment you took
your first breath, one fact became certain: your death was
inevitable. You are going to expend your life for something.
When it's over, when your life is spent, the only thing that
matters is whether you did anything with your life of genuine value.

Will you fall out of line with the rest and challenge the

status quo? Will you choose the road less traveled? Will you offer yourself before the Lord as a living sacrifice and walk the narrow road? I don't know about you, but I am tired of looking like everyone else. I am tired of conforming to and complying with the status quo. Christianity is radical by nature! It always has been and always will be. It upsets the complacency of the culture and resets what is considered normal.

It is time to find your cause! It is time to see the kingdom of God come to your home, school, family, friends, workplace, city, and nation. It's time to sail into the belly of the beast and overthrow the kingdom of darkness. It's time to fall out of line!

I can say, through the power of the Spirit, that wherever God can get a people that will come together in one accord and one mind in the word of God, the baptism of the Holy Ghost will fall upon them, like as at Cornelius' house.[1]

—William J. Seymour

Chapter 8

THE CLOUD THAT NEVER LIFTED

The Azusa Street Revival

*Behold, how good and how pleasant it is
for brothers to dwell together in unity!*

—Psalm 133:1

August 1906, Los Angeles, California

T HE REVIVAL MEETINGS at the little mission found at 312 Azusa Street were always powerful. This night would be no different. The atmosphere overflowed with great excitement and expectation. Everyone sensed that something powerful could happen at any moment.

People didn't come to Azusa Street to hear a man speak about God; they came to meet with God. Those familiar with the meetings entered the mission in quiet reverence. There was no time for idle words. Their thoughts were on spiritual things. The glory of the Lord was in the house, and they knew it. Some even claimed to see it.[2]

A curious black teenage boy named Thomas enthusiastically climbed to his feet atop a wooden bench, causing the rough redwood plank to bow under the combined weight of the fifteen-year-old and a dozen others who had crammed themselves onto the pew. Thomas was an inch shy of six

feet, yet even with his tall, slender frame he found it difficult to get a good view.

The ceilings of the Apostolic Faith Mission hung low,
so low that the second floor joists overhead could be easily
grasped with uplifted hands. That was especially true
from atop the makeshift pews that sat upon a dirt floor.[3]
This was the vantage point from which Thomas found
himself. It was a familiar position for the young man.
Ever since he had received the baptism of the Holy Spirit
in the first few weeks of the revival, he rarely missed an
opportunity to be at the mission. He was on fire for the
Lord and enjoyed watching the miracles that took place
every night.[4]

Thomas wasn't alone. Hundreds came each day into the
little mission that a few months earlier was just an old,
dilapidated two-story building. Then it was being used as a
barn to store lumber and keep animals. Now it was hosting
a growing revival. Azusa wasn't a prestigious sanctuary
filled with pretty, pious people; it was a simple warehouse
located on the wrong side of the tracks. Yet thousands from
different races and backgrounds willingly put aside their
prejudice and came, filled with either hunger or curiosity,
most times a little of both.

This night space inside was limited. Thomas supposed
there to be more than two hundred men and women
packed in the downstairs of the mission, with more upstairs
in the prayer room. A handful more were outside watching
through windows. The large crowd inside made the room
hot, and the smell of dirt and sweat filled the air. But
Thomas didn't mind.

The service itself had never actually started; it was
more or less a continuation of the previous one. Officially
the mission held three meetings a day, but the services

themselves just blended into one another. It had become one long revival service that would eventually last three years.[5] That's the way it was at the Apostolic Faith Mission on Azusa Street. Morning, noon, or night the doors were always open, and hungry believers could be found waiting on the Lord. Like the temple of old, the church was always open.

When Thomas had entered the building that night, several people were testifying. One after the next, people throughout the room stood to their feet and enthusiastically told about how they had received the Holy Spirit or been healed or saved.

As Thomas listened, a short man from a Mayan tribe in central Mexico stood and began to testify in his tribal tongue. His testimony was interpreted by a friend who had accompanied him to the meeting. He shared how he came to Azusa Street and heard a German woman preaching the gospel to him in his own language. He was astonished to hear someone speak so fluently a tongue he alone knew. She didn't understand what she was saying. She was simply speaking in tongues, but what she said was for him alone. He was convicted at once, and he surrendered his life to Jesus that very night.[6]

He jumped up and down shouting the only words in English he knew: "Jesus! Hallelujah! Jesus, Hallelujah! Jee-sus!"[7]

This wasn't the first time Thomas had heard a testimony like this. Like on the first Day of Pentecost, immigrants from nations all over the world would visit the revival and hear the wonders of God being declared in their own tongue. Each would fall under conviction and go running to the altar. This was just one of the many signs that validated this move of God.

Thomas watched as the excited Mayan man ran across

the room and laid hands on a sickly looking woman. She had been suffering from tuberculosis. Immediately she felt the power of God go through her body and was instantly healed. Jumping up to her feet, she picked up the testimony where the little man had left off.[8]

The excitement was contagious. Spontaneous praise broke out in the meeting. Some shouted, "Amen!" Others prayed in tongues. After a few minutes of rejoicing, the testimonies continued. This was Thomas's favorite part of the meeting. The testimonies could last for hours, but he didn't mind. He loved hearing the stories of what God was doing.

Everyone was treated as equals at Azusa Street. There was no platform to exalt one above another. All were on level ground. Even the benches along with various mismatched chairs were arranged around the room in the shape of a square so the people were facing one another. Anyone, regardless of race or age, could be used of God at any time to share a testimony, sing a song, or even bring the message.[9]

In the center of the room was the altar. It was made with a wooden plank suspended between two chairs. Men and women, both black and white, kneeled or laid in the dirt and sawdust at that altar.[10] Some were down of their own volition; others were overcome by the Spirit of God and lost the strength to stand. Some wept, some shook, and a few lay silently as if in a trance.

Because of the openness of the meetings, it was common to see a prideful man come into the building to publicly mock or scoff at the revival. Thomas had seen local pastors enter the building in such a way. No one would rebuke them or ask them to leave. They trusted the Holy Spirit to deal with them. The worshippers at Azusa would simply pray. Within minutes the prideful countenances of the scoffers would change. Their words would become confused, and conviction would overcome. They would be left with no choice but to run to the altar or for the door.[11]

People from all walks of life made the trip down to that altar. Doctors, lawyers, professors, and even pastors could be found kneeling in the dust alongside the drunk and destitute. Social status and class meant nothing there. God was in the house, and He was drawing men of every tribe and nation to Himself. People entered the building with humility, or the Spirit of the Lord humbled them.

No one directed the service. At best, William Seymour, the pastor of the mission, sought to simply steward and facilitate what the Holy Spirit was doing. Seymour was a stout thirty-six-year-old black man. He always wore an old black suit over a white button-up shirt and vest. He had a round face with a thick beard he had grown to cover the scars on his face from a near fatal bout of smallpox. That same illness had also left him blind in his left eye. He was a humble man yet carried himself with a quiet confidence.[12]

Seymour was a devout man of prayer who for the last hour had been sitting opposite Thomas partially hidden behind a simple wooden pulpit. The pulpit wasn't fancy. It had been pieced together from two wooden crates. Seymour would often sit behind the pulpit and hide his head inside the top crate.[13]

Visitors to the mission found the sight of a preacher hiding his head like an ostrich in the sand to be odd, but nothing at Azusa Street was like anything most people had been a part of. Thomas, like the rest of the regulars, was used to it. He often wondered what Seymour was doing, or more importantly, hearing inside that crate. More than once Thomas had sat next to Seymour and leaned in toward the box hoping to catch a glimpse inside. Thomas was fascinated by Seymour, as were most who attended the revival.[14]

The testimonies came to an end, and a reverent silence fell across the room. It lasted for several minutes. Seymour quietly removed his head from the crate and stood to his feet. He called for those in attendance to sing in the Spirit. A middle-aged black woman sitting near the center of the room began to sing in tongues with a beautiful, loud voice. Another joined in with her, then another. Soon the sound of dozens of voices all singing in different languages began to fill the room, all in harmony with the other.[15]

The sound was out of this world. No one sang the same words, yet the song itself seemed the same. It was as if the song service was suddenly being conducted from heaven and the angels had joined in with the earthly choir. The whole mission came alive with the manifest presence of the Lord.

Thomas perked up. He knew that when the saints all sang together in one new song, the power of God would manifest. He pulled himself up to his tiptoes and leaned forward from atop the bench. His eyes, once fixed solely on Seymour, began to wander around the room. The atmosphere was heaven on earth. That is when he noticed the cloud. All around the room the whole place seemed to be filled with a dense cloud—a visible, physical cloud.

This wasn't the first time Thomas had seen it. The saints called it the Shekinah glory. Many claimed to see it every time they came into the mission. It never left. Sometimes it was merely a mist; other times it would be so thick you could lie down in it.[16]

The first person to have seen the cloud was an evangelist named Frank Bartleman. He was a thirty-five-year-old

white man who had been attending the revival since
the beginning. He said the cloud first came into a prayer
meeting he was hosting in his home.[17] He along with several displaced members from a local church had gathered
there to pray for revival.

They had all been attending the First Baptist Church led
by Pastor Joseph Smale. Smale had visited the revival in
Wales and was stirred by what he saw. When he returned
to Los Angeles, he began to encourage his church to contend for revival in their own city. For a time the leaders
of the church humored him, but soon they tired of all
the revival talk and desired to return to the "old way" of
doing things. Smale couldn't go back to the status quo,
so he resigned his position immediately. He along with
Bartleman and several members of the congregation began
to meet together regularly.[18]

Bartleman had wondered if he and the church members had behaved pridefully, but the presence of the cloud
during the prayer meetings convinced him they were on
the right course and that revival would soon come. It was
his desire to follow the cloud wherever it led. It led him to
Azusa Street.

God doesn't move according to our plans, but He always
responds to our prayers. Revival did come, but not where
Bartleman thought it would. It broke out on April 6, 1906,
on the other side of town at another prayer meeting taking
place in the home of a black couple who lived on Bonnie
Brae Street. Within days large crowds were gathering outside the home. Bartleman later remarked that had God
visited Smale's church first, it would likely have kept the
Mexicans, blacks, and immigrants out. However, God in
His wisdom sent it to an unlikely place first, and in doing
so brought Pentecost to all.[19]

It didn't take long before Bartleman and many others from the church began attending the prayer meetings on Bonnie Brae Street and experienced the fresh flames of the revival they had prayed for. The large crowds at Bonnie Brae made finding a more suitable building necessary. The Lord led William Seymour to the property located at 312 Azusa Street.

The first service at Azusa Street took place Easter weekend and never really ended. The meetings blended into one another for more than three years. Bartleman said the Shekinah glory was always present there. He even heard others share that they had seen the glory appear like a fire over the building itself.[20]

Thomas was one of those. One night after hearing a friend talk about seeing flames over the mission, he ran outside to see it for himself. What he saw looked like fire coming down from heaven into the building. There was also fire going up from the building, and it met the fire coming down.[21]

That friend Thomas heard talking about seeing flames over the mission was named David Garcia. He was the nineteen-year-old son of Mexican immigrants, and he lived one mile from the mission. He had seen the fire more than once as he walked to the mission. One night Garcia came running into the mission and found Bartleman. He had passed the train depot located a half mile from the mission.

"Frank, you have to see what is happening at the train station!"

Together the two ran down to the station and found people lying all over the station. Some were shaking; others were speaking in tongues. When a train would arrive, as soon as the passengers stepped foot on the ground, they were suddenly hit with conviction. Garcia had heard that this had been happening all day long.[22]

Bartleman himself had experienced something like this before, but this was the first time he had seen the glory affect so many so far from the mission. It was as if the Spirit of God had drawn a "dead line" around the mission. When men came within the line, they were seized with conviction.[23]

It was during these times when the glory was so noticeably present that greater signs and wonders would take place in the building. As Thomas watched the cloud while standing on his pew, he knew this was going to be one of those nights.

The sound of singing began to lull, and Seymour moved to the opposite side of the room. There was a section of people who were suffering from physical problems. Seymour raised his arm toward them and boldly said, "You want to see a miracle over there? Every one of you within a few minutes is going to be up and walking in the name of Jesus."[24]

It didn't take minutes. It was instant. Thomas could not believe his eyes or his ears. The sound of bones snapping and cracking back into place filled the room. It was just as Seymour had said. Everyone was healed.

How could they not be? They were all standing within the Shekinah glory. They were literally breathing the atmosphere of heaven into their lungs. It would have been impossible to remain the way they came.

That night Thomas had a front-row seat to the miraculous. Like so many nights at the revival, it was an encounter he would never forget.

IN ONE PLACE, IN ONE ACCORD

The Azusa Street Revival took place over one hundred years ago; the saints who participated have passed away, yet their stories live on. Their testimonies offer a glimpse into what the revival was like and stir hunger in anyone who has ears to hear. Like all things passed down over decades, some things are sure to be embellished or changed. However, one thing that remains consistent in the writings of saints such as Frank Bartleman, in the Azusa Street papers, and even in the oral stories is the Shekinah glory—the manifest presence of the Lord.

For more than three years the cloud of God's glory rested on the house. Some claimed to see it; everyone felt it. They said the cloud never lifted—it was always present! Just as it was in the days of old, God filled His house with the cloud of His glory! It attracted hundreds of thousands from all around the world. They came, following the cloud, and left filled with God's Spirit.

There are over six hundred million Pentecostals on earth today. Every single one of them can trace their roots back to 312 Azusa Street. Though the building no longer remains, the fire that started there certainly does. That fire spread from Los Angles all around the world. The Pentecostal church continues to be the fastest growing segment of Christianity in the world.[25] As it was in the days that followed the first Pentecost, so has it been in the days that followed the Azusa Street Revival. The fire of God is impossible to contain. It spreads, transforming everything in its wake. Those who wish to find it need only humble themselves and come before the Lord.

Frank Bartleman was right. God chose an unlikely location to send revival, but in doing so He sent a clear message.

The mission itself became a sign to all who would enter. It called out, "Humble thyself!"

That message was woven through every part of the revival, including the building. The mission was first a two-story church that was constructed by the First African Methodist Episcopal Church in Los Angeles. Their sanctuary was on the upper floor while the lower floor was used to stable the horses of the congregation. However, when the area around Azusa Street began to transition, the church moved in search of a more desirable location. They renovated the old sanctuary into apartments while the first floor continued to be used for storage and a stable. By 1906 the building had fallen into disrepair and was listed for sale. Seymour leased the building from the former church for eight dollars a month. He chose to move the revival into the bottom floor. There an old stable, a room that used to house farm animals, would provide shelter to this fledging move of God.[26] Looking back, it was a fitting choice.

The following was written in *The Apostolic Faith*, the newspaper of the Azusa Street Revival:

> It has been said of the work in Los Angeles that He was "born in a manger and resurrected in a barn." Many are praising God for the old barn-like building on Azusa Street, and the plain old plank beside which they kneeled in the sawdust when God saved, sanctified and baptized them with the Holy Ghost. Those who know God feel His presence as soon as they cross the threshold.[27]

God certainly loves visiting humble stables! Two thousand years ago, when God stepped out of heaven and came to earth, He didn't come to a palace; He came to a stable.

It was a manger, not a throne, that became a resting place for God's own Son. Had Jesus been born into a life of opulence, the common man would have never been afforded the opportunity to come close to Him. However, since Jesus was born among the lowest of creatures, the lowest among men could come to worship at His feet. Anyone and everyone was welcome to seek Him out, from simple shepherds to wealthy wise men.

The same could be said of the Azusa Street Revival. People from all walks of life, denominations, races, occupations, and social classes were welcomed at the mission. The only requirement was to come in humble unity. Everything about this move of God, from the building to the services, demanded it. *The Apostolic Faith* said it like this:

> Some have come from long distances to this spot, directed of the Lord, and the humble have always been greatly blest. The work began among the colored people. God baptized several sanctified wash women with the Holy Ghost, who have been much used of Him. The first white woman to receive the Pentecost and gift of tongues in Los Angeles was Mrs. Evans who is now in the work in Oakland. Since then multitudes have come. God makes no difference in nationality. Ethiopians, Chinese, Indians, Mexicans, and other nationalities worship together.[28]

There was unity in the house, and as such the Shekinah glory manifest itself in their midst. Just as God filled the temple with His glory in the days of Solomon, He once again filled the mission with a cloud that never lifted. For more than three years the presence of the Lord rested at Azusa Street, and everyone was invited to come and worship together.

Red, yellow, black, and white—they all came to this

humble mission. This was a remarkable and unlikely accomplishment. America was a deeply divided nation at the time. Racism and segregation ruled supreme in all corners of the country, except at Azusa Street. Frank Bartleman wrote: "The 'color line' was washed away in the blood."[29] A. S. Worrell declared:

> The "Azusa" work had rediscovered the blood of Christ to the church at that time...divine love was wonderfully manifest in the meetings. They would not even allow an unkind word said against their opposers, or the churches. The message was the love of God. It was a sort of "first love" of the early church returned. The baptism as we received it in the beginning did not allow us to think, speak, or hear evil of any man.[30]

Pentecost came to Azusa Street as it came in the Book of Acts. The Word of God says, "When the Day of Pentecost had fully come, they were all with one accord in one place" (Acts 2:1, NKJV). When the early disciples were unified with one heart, the anointing was poured out. William Seymour wrote several years after the Azusa revival, "Wherever God can get a people that will come together in one accord and one mind in the word of God, the baptism of the Holy Ghost will fall upon them."[31]

If we truly desire to see revival in our day, we must learn the lesson of Azusa Street and seek a place of true unity in the body. The moment that blessed unity is rediscovered, the cloud will return! God is not looking for *another* church; He's looking for *one* church!

Today the Spirit of God is passing many by because they are too full of self or offense to be filled with anything else. Pride and selfishness blind and bind the saints from experiencing the outpouring that comes upon humility and unity. Learn the lesson from 312 Azusa Street. There a building that was once a stately church had to become a humble stable before it became a house filled with the Shekinah glory. The original congregation abandoned the building in search of better surroundings; little did they know that what man found unattractive, God found irresistible. Perhaps the move of God we seek isn't found in another place but a different position.

> God is not looking for *another* church; He's looking for *one* church!

Many ask where the miracles are and why revival tarries. They wonder where the cloud has gone. The answer is simple. As long as we remain separate and selfish, the Spirit cannot come. Imagine the divine possibilities when all of God's people in a community take down every wall that divides them and walk together in unity. Imagine the shift that will take place within your city when churches stand together united in a common cause and with a common voice.

There is an extreme blessing that is *commanded* by God to come upon such unity. Psalm 133 says:

> Behold, how good and how pleasant it is for brothers to dwell together in unity! It is like precious oil upon the head, that runs down on the beard—even Aaron's beard—and going down to the collar of his garments; as the dew of Hermon, that descends upon the mountains of Zion, for there the LORD has commanded the blessing, even life forever.

Scripture says God has *commanded* the blessing. He has already given the order to release the oil of anointing wherever unity is present. If we want the cloud back, we need only bring unity back!

This is what the disciples found when they were gathered "with one accord in one place" (Acts 2:1, NKJV). The promised blessing of the Spirit of God came in such force it sounded like a violent wind. Tongues of fire landed upon their heads, and these men and women went on to shake the world. (See Acts 2:1–4.) The saints at Azusa Street found that blessing as well. They laid aside their divisions of race, class, and denomination, and the Spirit of the Lord descended in power and the cloud of His presence filled the house. Can it happen again? It will if we can heed the lesson of Azusa Street.

In the later part of 1906 a holiness preacher from Dunn, North Carolina, named G. B. Cashwell came to Azusa Street. He had read some of the stories Frank Bartleman had printed, and the stories stirred a hunger in the preacher for his own Pentecost. He began seeking the Lord for the baptism of the Spirit but did not receive it. The frustrated pastor finally decided his only choice was to go to the revival itself. He boarded a train and spent six days traveling the length of the nation. He fasted and prayed all three thousand miles. The man came hungry and ready, but still he didn't receive the baptism of the Holy Spirit. Something stood between him and the blessing.

Cashwell arrived in Los Angeles on a Sunday and immediately went to Azusa Street with great expectation. However, when he entered the mission, the scene was not what he expected. Being a white preacher from the South, he found the mixing of the races to be too much for his sensibility and left offended. He could not bring himself to allow a black man to lay hands on him in prayer.

It seemed to have been a wasted trip. That night he

wrestled with the Lord in prayer. He came to the conclusion that if he wanted to experience Pentecost, he would have to crucify his flesh. Remember, sacrifice fuels the fires of revival! He went back to the mission and straight to the altar. He prostrated himself in the dirt and sawdust and repented before the Lord.

William Seymour came and laid hands on the white preacher, and Cashwell was immediately baptized in the Holy Spirit with the evidence of tongues. The man's life was forever changed because he took down the wall that stood between him and the blessing. Imagine the sight: Cashwell on his knees at the altar next to a black brother, both seeking the baptism.

Upon such unity, the anointing was poured out, and it ran down from the top of the preacher's head to the bottom of his feet. Cashwell knew there was something at Azusa Street he had to have. Once he resolved to let nothing stand his way, he removed the wall separating him from it and received an impartation.

God has commanded a blessing to come upon the unity of the brethren. However, as long as division and disunity are allowed to remain on the inside, revival will continue to remain on the outside. Separation and segregation will always hinder impartation. Yes, there are a multitude of things that can divide us, but there need only be one thing to unite us.

Cashwell came to Azusa hungry for the things of God, but until that hunger became greater than his own prejudice, he couldn't experience the blessing God had for him. Once he was willing to repent and kneel down beside his brother, the blessing came.

After spending six days at the mission, Cashwell made his way back to North Carolina. There he wasted no time.

He rented a warehouse and began holding his own services. His meetings became known as Azusa East.[32] Cashwell brought the cloud from the West Coast to the East Coast.

Where is the cloud today? Why has the promised blessing tarried? Is it due to a lack of churches within our community or a lack of unity within our churches? We certainly have no shortage of churches, but we are severely lacking revival. If God promises to visit unity with an outpouring, perhaps it's time we start taking down walls and kneeling in the dirt and sawdust with our brothers. As I said, God is not looking for another church; He is looking for *one* church.

Revival is something altogether different from evangelism on its highest level. . . . Revival is a moving of God in the community and suddenly the community becomes God conscious before a word is said by any man representing any special effort.[1]

—**Duncan Campbell, 1968**

Chapter 9

THEY CAME WITHOUT
BEING INVITED

The Hebrides Revival

*For I will pour water on him who is thirsty, and floods
on the dry ground; I will pour out My Spirit on your
descendants, and My blessing on your offspring.*

—Isaiah 44:3

December 7, 1949, Island of Lewis, Scotland

T HE CLOCK HAD just struck 11:00 p.m. and the prayer
meeting had just come to a close when the local
blacksmith burst through the back doors of the church to
find the reverend, Duncan Campbell.

"Mr. Campbell," he cried out, "something wonderful has
happened. Oh, we were praying that God would pour water
on the thirsty and floods upon the dry ground and listen,
He's done it! He's done it!"[2]

It was true. Revival had come. It came suddenly and powerfully. It fell from heaven like a torrential flood in the most
inexplicable and glorious fashion. The skies above opened,
and the Spirit of God was poured out. The entire land was
now awash in the presence of the Lord. There was no doubt

this was a sovereign move of God, and no one, not even Mr. Campbell, would be able to take credit for it.

Campbell had just arrived a few hours earlier upon the Isle of Lewis, just off the coast of Scotland. For him it had been a long day of travel. It was late that evening when his steamer had pulled up to the pier. He hoped to make his way to bed soon and get some rest before a week of ministry.

Waiting on Mr. Campbell at the pier was Reverend James Murray MacKay and two of his elders. MacKay was pastor of a church in the village of Barvas. He was a humble, sincere, and faith-filled man. When Campbell stepped off the boat, he and the two elders went right to him and reached out their hands. Wasting no time with pleasantries, one of the elders looked the evangelist in the eyes said, "Mr. Campbell, I would like to ask you a question before you leave this pier: Are you walking with God?"

Campbell was struck by the elder's boldness. It was immediately obvious to Campbell that this was a very serious man who meant business with the Lord. No doubt this would be an extraordinary time of ministry. He looked back and said, "Well, I think I can say this: that I fear God."

The elder paused for a moment then said, "That will do."[3]

It was MacKay who had invited Campbell to come to the Island of Lewis. Campbell was expecting to stay just a few days; little did he know he would be staying for the next three years. Neither the pastor nor the evangelist was in charge; it was the Spirit of God who was orchestrating this revival.

The outpouring came as a response to the prayers of two elderly sisters, Peggy and Christine Smith. Peggy was eighty-four years old and blind while her sister was eighty-two and dealt with severe arthritis. Though weakened by age, these two women were strong in spirit.[4] Lately they had become increasingly burdened by the condition of their local church. The attendance had dwindled, and not a single young person attended the services. Rather than complain, they chose to pray.

They had read the forty-fourth chapter of Isaiah, and now the third verse seemed to leap from the pages and grip them: "I will pour water upon him that is thirsty, and floods upon the dry ground" (kjv).

"That is the promise," they said. "We believe that God is a covenant-keeping God who must be true to His covenant engagements. He has made a promise, and He must fulfill the promise."[5]

They had no doubt God would pour water on the dry and thirsty ground if they would sow their prayers into it. The two sisters had their assignment from the Lord. They would commit two nights a week to praying for the fulfillment of the promise. Every Tuesday and Friday they locked themselves up in their humble cottage. They would get on their knees at ten o'clock in the evening to pray through the night, oftentimes until three or four in the morning.

It was during one of these times of prayer that Peggy had a vision. Though she had lost her natural eyesight, her spiritual eyes were still bright. She saw the church packed wall to wall with people. There was not an empty seat to be found. In the room were hundreds of young people all crying out to God. Behind the pulpit she saw a minister whom she did not know. The vision so shook her that she immediately called her pastor and asked him to come to her home at once.

When Reverend MacKay arrived, Peggy could hardly

contain herself. She explained how the Lord had spoken to her and her sister from Isaiah 44 and that they had been praying two nights each week. She then shared the vision and challenged the minister, "You must do something about it!"[6]

MacKay knew the two ladies to be godly women. He agreed with Peggy and chose to follow their lead. He called for the elders of the church to come to pray for revival with him every Tuesday and Friday night. They met and prayed in a barn near the church, where they could stay warm.

It was late November, and at that point the men had been meeting together for over a month. On this particular night Pastor MacKay was kneeling before the Lord, reading Isaiah 44 again to himself and pleading the promise God gave, "I will pour water on him that is thirsty, floods upon the dry ground!"[7]

At that a young deacon in the church stood up and read aloud from Psalm 24: "Who shall ascend into the hill of the LORD? or who shall stand in his holy place? He that hath clean hands, and a pure heart; who hath not lifted up his soul unto vanity, nor sworn deceitfully. He shall receive the blessing from the LORD, and righteousness from the God of his salvation" (vv. 3–5, KJV).

The young man then closed his Bible and gently placed it on his seat. He looked sternly into the faces of his fellow brothers and said, "It seems to me to be so much humbug to be praying as we are praying, to be waiting as we are waiting, if we ourselves are not rightly related to God." Then he lifted his two hands to heaven and shouted to the Lord, "God, are my hands clean? Is my heart pure?"[8]

He got no further than that before he fell straight to the ground like a man knocked out cold in a boxing ring. He lay there on the ground in a trance. The leaders in the room didn't have time to ponder what this might mean, as the Spirit of God came so suddenly upon the prayer meeting. The minister and the deacons were gripped with holy fear and godly conviction. That night the men began confessing their sins before the Lord and fully surrendering their lives into His service.

The power of God that broke out that night in the barn swept through the church the following day. The whole of the congregation was suddenly awakened to the reality and nearness of God. The following week, very little work was being done on the farms, in the factories, or in the shops. The men and women of the church found themselves drawn to prayer. Everyone was gripped by thoughts of eternity. It was apparent God was beginning to move.

As news of the outbreak reached the two sisters, they once again sent for the minister. They were pleased to hear how God was answering their prayers. Peggy reminded her pastor of the vision she had seen and said, "I think you ought to invite someone to the parish. I cannot give a name, but God must have someone in His mind because we saw a strange man in the pulpit, and that man must be somewhere."[9]

That same week Reverend MacKay went to a convention in Scotland and met a God-fearing young man whom he invited to the parish. The man declined and suggested that MacKay invite Duncan Campbell, a fifty-one-year-old Scottish preacher who of late had developed a great following in Ireland and Scotland. MacKay invited Campbell to the parish to conduct a series of meetings for ten days.

When the invitation arrived, Campbell replied that his schedule was booked for several months, and it would be the following year before he could come to the island.

When he received Campbell's reply, MacKay went to the sisters and told them the story. Peggy replied, "That is what man is saying, but God has said otherwise, and the man, whoever he is, is going to be here within ten days."[10] Ten days later Campbell was standing on the pier with Reverend MacKay.

Once Campbell was on the pier, MacKay turned to the evangelist and said, "I know, Mr. Campbell, that you are very tired. You have been traveling all day by train to begin with and then by steamer. And I am sure that you are ready for your supper and ready for your bed. But I wonder if you would be prepared to address a meeting in the parish church at 9 o'clock tonight on our way home. It will be a short meeting and then we will make for the manse and you will get your supper and your bed and rest until tomorrow evening."[11]

Though Campbell was tired from his journey, he felt he had no choice but to oblige. When they arrived at the church, Campbell was surprised to find nearly three hundred people gathered for this small prayer service. The presence of God was immediately evident in the church. The people prayed in quiet reverence, with their minds set on God. Campbell greeted the audience and spoke for over an hour. Nothing remarkable took place. Then, being very tired from the day of travel, he dismissed himself and proceeded to leave. It was a quarter before eleven o'clock.

Campbell started making his way down the aisle toward the door, along with the young deacon who had read Psalm 24 and prayed so passionately in the barn. But the deacon now stood in the aisle, looking up to the heavens, and said, "God, You can't fail us. God, You can't fail us. You promised to pour water on the thirsty and floods upon the dry ground—God, You can't fail us!"[12]

He then fell to his knees in the aisle and began praying fervently before falling to the floor once again as if in a trance. The sight normally would have caused Campbell some alarm, but he didn't have time to think about it. Suddenly the back door of the church burst open, and there, stunned in the threshold, was the blacksmith.

"Something wonderful has happened. Oh, we were praying that God would pour water on the thirsty and floods upon the dry ground and listen, He's done it! He's done it!"[13]

Outside the doors of the church, nearly six hundred people were waiting to come in. Where had six hundred people come from at such a late hour? What had happened? Duncan Campbell had to know what caused so many people to come at once.

Many in the crowd were young men and women, mostly under the age of twenty-five. They had been nearby partying at a dance when suddenly the power of God fell upon the room. It was an intense spirit of conviction that descended within the hall. The band stopped playing, and the people stopped dancing. The room became repulsive, and no one wanted to remain inside. They left the dance and went outside. There they noticed the lights on at the church, and they came at once.

The rest of the six hundred had come from their homes. Whole families who had already been in bed were suddenly roused from their sleep. They didn't know why, but they felt compelled to get to the church. They dressed as quickly as they could and made their way there. Now they all were standing outside the church in the cold air wishing to come in. Six hundred came to the church without being invited, at least not by men. They didn't understand it, but it was the Spirit of God that drew them.

The blacksmith turned to Campbell and said, "I think that we should sing a psalm."[14] At that the doors to the church were opened, and the entire congregation began to sing as the new group entered and filled the sanctuary. Within minutes the church was filled to capacity. Duncan Campbell was speechless. He was suddenly standing in a packed house without a single empty seat. It was exactly as Peggy had seen in her vision.

It was just now midnight, and the church was filled. Men and women knelt at the front of the church and around the altar. Others knelt in their seats. Some lay prostrate before the Lord. No one was silent; everyone was either crying out for mercy or praising the Lord.

Duncan Campbell made his way back toward the front of the church. In front of the pulpit he walked past a young lady who moments before had been at the dance. She was a teacher in the local grammar school. Now she was at the altar, lying on the ground. She kept crying out to the Lord, "Oh, God, is there mercy for me? Oh, God, is there mercy for me?"[15]

There wasn't much Campbell could do. There was no need to give an altar call and no need to preach. The Lord Himself was obviously doing the work. The meeting continued until four o'clock in the morning when a very tired Duncan Campbell felt he could go on no longer. He asked for someone to take him to the parsonage so that he might rest. As he was leaving the church, a young man came to him and said, "Mr. Campbell, I would like you to go to the police station."

"The police station? What's wrong?"

"Oh," he said, "There's nothing wrong but there must be at least 400 people gathered around the police station just now."[16]

The station was about a mile from the church, and Campbell had to see what was taking place. He, the young man, and a few others from the church began to walk toward the station. As they made their way down the road, Campbell heard the sounds of praying coming from somewhere nearby. He walked over to investigate and found four young men bent upon their knees crying out to God. The smell of alcohol surrounded the men, and it was apparent they had been at the dance but had not come to the church with the rest. Now they were by the roadside at an altar of their own.

After praying with the men, Campbell continued toward the police station, completely unprepared for what awaited him. It was just as the man said: four hundred people were gathered outside the station. The scene was very similar to what has happening at the church. People stood, knelt, and lay on the ground, weeping and wailing. They were all crying out to God for mercy.

Duncan Campbell had never seen or heard of anything like this happening before. Again, he realized there was no need to preach. The work had already begun in their hearts. Just like the four men on the side of the road, the people at the police station were already praying to God. Campbell heard one man cry out in painful agony, "Oh, God, hell is too good for me! Hell is too good for me!"[17]

That night hundreds were born again in to the kingdom of God right in front of the police station. Campbell didn't have to lead a single one to Jesus. The Lord brought them to Himself.

REVIVAL MEANS GOD'S ARRIVAL!

The Hebrides Revival lasted for three years. It swept through not only the island of Lewis but also all of the Hebrides

Islands. Within a matter of weeks every church was filled to capacity. In most cases, the majority of people came to church already saved. As it was that first night, God Himself gave the altar call. He called them by the roadside and out in the fields. He called them in their homes and as they moved about the city. During this revival it wasn't uncommon to find groups of people gathering together and suddenly seeing revival break out in their midst.

The Hebrides Revival changed Campbell's understanding of what a move of God looked like. Revival could no longer be viewed as a series of evangelistic meetings or special services. It was supernatural and, as such, something man could not manufacture or reproduce. He said, "Revival is something altogether different from evangelism on its highest level.... Revival is a moving of God in the community and suddenly the community becomes God conscious before a word is said by any man."[18] In other words, revival means God's arrival!

Revival is a word that is used a lot in the church. It is passed around without much thought as to how someone might define it. It's not uncommon to hear two people use the word but have two completely different interpretations of it.

So when you talk about revival, what do you really mean? When you pray for revival, what exactly are you praying for? If you are like me, you most likely envision the answer to your prayers in your mind. Ephesians 3:20 tells us that God is able to "exceedingly abundantly beyond all that we ask or imagine."

I have a pretty active imagination and like to picture the answer to my prayers. Plus, if Paul tell us that God is able to answer those prayers, "exceedingly" and "abundantly" beyond what I can imagine, I want to give God something to work with. Don't just imagine little things. Stretch your imagination and your faith, and expect God to do even more than you ever thought!

When I pray for revival, I imagine it moving like fire through my church and community. I envision the altars filled with friends and family repenting before the Lord and getting right with God. I hear the cries and see the tears that soak the carpet in the front of the church. I imagine my city and cities across the nation suddenly awakening to God. I see bars and strip clubs closing down as churches are filled up. I see those churches filled with excitement and hear the sounds of praise as people shout and dance before the Lord.

I believe the next great move of God will have incredible signs and wonders as believers are once again filled with true Pentecostal power. Certainly revival must bring great physical healing. The lame will walk, the deaf will hear, and the blind will see. Cancer will be a forgotten thing, and sickness will no longer plague the land. When I pray for revival, that is what I imagine!

Pastor John Kilpatrick, who led Brownsville Assembly of God during the Pensacola Outpouring, has spoken often about his understanding of revival before the outpouring hit his congregation on Father's Day 1995. His church had prayed earnestly for revival for a year before that day. Surely if a church was praying for revival for so long, they must have had a vision of what they were seeking. What did he envision?

Pastor Kilpatrick said he thought it would be something much as he had seen before: several weeks of extended meetings and hundreds of salvations. He had an idea of what revival looked like, but God had another. Pastor Kilpatrick never would have imagined God would do something so great. In the end, that revival lasted five years, impacted millions of people all over the world, and brought more than 150,000 souls into the kingdom. God exceeded his expectations and rewrote his understanding of revival.[19]

Oh, Lord, rewrite our understanding of revival as well! Revival is not merely salvations, times of refreshing, great miracles, and the exponential growth of the church. Yes, all those things and more are certainly welcomed and should be desired, but they in themselves are not revival. Those things are the secondary consequence to revival. They are the fruit that follows a genuine awakening. Revival itself is something far more powerful than we understand.

Revival is when the eternal, all-consuming presence of the Lord comes into His church. Revival is God's arrival! It is when the King of kings enters a community and is allowed to inhabit His throne with absolute authority. It is the moment when you become alive in God and He becomes real to you. That is something altogether different from what we must think or imagine about revival!

Consider the drastic difference between asking God for salvations or church growth and having a true encounter with the manifest presence of God. Most people would likely welcome the former and run from the latter. Our notion of God is built on stories and ideas of what He is like. The sobering truth is, God is far more incredible and awesome than we could ever imagine. Hebrews 10:31 says, "It is a fearful thing to fall into the hands of the living God."

Our view of God is too small. Were God to manifest Himself before you and expose you to the fullness of His glory, it would be both life-altering and life-ending, for no man sees God and lives! Our God is an all-consuming fire and dwells in unapproachable light (Heb. 12:29; 1 Tim 6:16). Yes, it is a fearful thing to come before Him!

During the revival in Hebrides the whole of the island was awakened at once to this reality of God. The God of heaven came down and rested upon the island. Men and women found themselves drawn to Him. They responded to His drawing, and once in His presence they became painfully aware of how great God was and how far away from Him they were. That realization transformed everything, not just for the individual but for the whole community.

Did Peggy and Christine Smith know what they were asking for when they began praying for revival? I can't imagine they could have. They wanted to see their church changed, but when God came, everything changed!

Do we truly want revival? Revival is costly and changes everything. When God arrives, He upends and usurps our agendas. Our schedules will be inconvenienced; our selfish desires will become inconsequential. There is no room for pride or the flesh in revival. Egos become casualties, and sin is dealt with swiftly. His holiness touches us, and by His fire we are purified. Revival means death to the old so it can bring new life.

Is that what we really want? Is it not far more convenient to pray for growth in our churches than to relinquish control of His church? Is it not easier to pray for the salvation of a loved one than it is to allow God full use of our voice to share the message of salvation with them? Is it not far more convenient to pray for God to bless the poor than it is to sell all we have and give to them? This is the difference between seeking the hand of God and seeking God Himself. One merely wants God's blessing; the other desires His Lordship.

I wonder, do we really want revival? I am stirred as I think about the powerful, sovereign move that took place in the Hebrides. There the Spirit of God descended upon a land, and mankind was overcome by the sheer weight of His presence. No one could take credit for this outpouring. It was not manufactured or manipulated. Even the evangelist found himself at a loss for work. God poured out His Spirit, and man was simply the recipient.

> There is a cost to see a move of God—more than prayer, or rearranged schedules or agendas. It's total and complete surrender to the Lordship of Jesus.

The night revival broke out, four hundred people were inexplicably drawn together outside the police station. It was early in the morning. It seemed as if they had been supernaturally drawn to this location. The Spirit of the Lord, like a magnet, had pulled on hundreds of lost souls and brought them there. They said they came seeking information. Perhaps there was more to it than that.

Right next to the police station was a little cottage that belonged to the two elderly sisters. These sisters had prayed for revival into the wee hours of the morning every Tuesday and Friday. Revival always comes as a response to the prayers of God's people. These sisters had sacrificed in prayer for months to see God pour out His Spirit upon the dry and thirsty ground. That night their prayers were answered right outside their door!

There is a cost to see a move of God—more than prayer, or rearranged schedules or agendas. It's total and complete surrender to the Lordship of Jesus. It is a steep price to pay, but nothing else is more worthy. The exchanging of our kingdom for God's kingdom is incomparable. Though it hurts to surrender to it, though we know the flesh can scarcely bear it, still we cry out for it. We welcome it because we are assured that God's shaking "signifies the removal of those things that can be shaken, things that are created, so that only those things that cannot be shaken will remain" (Heb. 12:27).

Let the shaking begin! In the coming revival God will be reestablishing His authority and glory upon the church. He will be returning the awe of His holiness to His people. As the writer of Hebrews continues, "Therefore, since we are receiving a kingdom that cannot be moved, let us be gracious, by which we may serve God acceptably with reverence and godly fear. For our God is a consuming fire" (vv. 28–29).

I challenge you to shift your attention in your prayers for revival. Instead of solely seeking the fruit of revival, seek the sovereign God of revival. See Him taking His rightful place upon the throne of your heart. Surrender it fully to Him so that He alone may reign.

In order for you to have a crown up there, you must live for Christ down here. To put on a crown up there, you must put on a cross down here. When you stand before Jesus, you will want a crown—a glorious crown—to lay at his feet in worship.[1]

—Steve Hill, 1999

Chapter 10

GOD IS IN A HURRY

The Brownsville Revival

*Look, I am coming quickly. Hold firmly what you
have, so that no one may take your crown.*

—Revelation 3:11

Thursday, June 29, 1995, Pensacola, Florida

W HAT ARE YOU doing Lord?" Amy asked.
"I'm cleaning you out," was His reply.[2]
Though she didn't fully understand what was happening,
one thing was certain—life for Amy Elizabeth Ward would
never be the same.

It was three thirty in the morning, and Amy was just getting up on her feet. For the past three hours she had been
powerfully moved upon by the Spirit of God at the altar at
Brownsville Assembly of God. Her older sister, Alison, had
been there at her side the whole time. In fact, it was Alison
who had brought her to the altar six hours earlier. Alison
had hoped and prayed Amy would have an encounter with
the presence of God, but even this was more than she could
have ever imagined.[3]

Before that night Amy was a rebellious teenage girl who
lived for the weekends when she would party hard with

her friends.[4] She showed little concern for others and only cared about what made her happy. This was not at all how she had been raised. Amy and Alison grew up in a well-respected and disciplined household. Their mother was a godly woman and a schoolteacher. Their father was a doctor. Amy's mom had tried her best to raise her girls in the fear of the Lord. She constantly encouraged them to do the right thing and walk the straight-and-narrow path. Yet despite all her mother's efforts, Amy rebelled; her heart and eyes were fully set on the world.[5]

Obviously, spending long nights at church was not how Amy originally planned to spend her summer, but that was before revival broke out. It started just one week earlier at their home church, Brownsville Assembly of God. Brownsville was a large, prestigious church that resided in the historic but now run-down business district of Pensacola. The church had chosen to remain even as the area went into decline. Recently they had completed construction on a beautiful two-thousand-seat sanctuary. The new red-brick campus took up a city block and was the one shining gem in an otherwise run-down part of town. Little did Brownsville know that their presence in the community would soon bring transformation not only to Pensacola but to the nations as well.[6]

The revival began on Father's Day when missionary and evangelist Steve Hill was invited to speak during the morning service. It was unusual for a senior pastor such as John Kilpatrick to give up his pulpit on such an important holiday. However, he had just lost his mother and was still mourning her passing. The grieving pastor welcomed the opportunity for a break from preaching. Steve Hill was a familiar face to Brownsville. He had spoken there a few times in the past. But something was noticeably different about him this Sunday.[7]

Steve was a fiery preacher with intense blue eyes that burned with a passion for the lost and the Lord. He spoke that morning from Psalm 77:11–12, which says, "I shall remember the deeds of the LORD; surely I will remember Your wonders of old. I will meditate on all Your work and muse on Your deeds" (NAS). Steve said, "This may be Father's Day, but friends, the Lord is going somewhere today.... We are going to look back and say, I remember Father's Day of 1993. I remember 1994, but let me talk to you about [Father's Day] 1995. I'll never forget that Sunday. I will never forget what happened to me on that day. We will remember the deeds of the Lord." The preacher then shared about a powerful encounter he'd recently had with the Lord. He said that ever since that experience, everything in his ministry had changed.[8]

Steve spoke for another forty-five minutes before giving an altar call for salvation. Seven individuals responded to the appeal. Steve asked for prayer workers to come lead the people to the cross and then invited all those who wanted a fresh encounter with the Lord to come forward. There were nearly eighteen hundred people in attendance that morning. More than half responded to the call for prayer; the other half took the opportunity to dismiss themselves. They left too soon.[9]

Steve walked down the steps from the pulpit and began working his way through the crowd, laying hands on one person after the next. His voice bellowed across the sanctuary. "Touch him, Jesus!" he cried as he laid his hand on one man. "Fresh touch," he said to another. "More, Lord!" he prayed for yet another. Steve's voice was forceful, but his touch was gentle. He barely laid his fingers on the foreheads of the people as he prayed for them. Yet many were powerfully touched by the presence of God. They fell to the ground as if a great weight had fallen on them from overhead.[10]

John Kilpatrick had never seen anything quite like this in his church before. Originally he wasn't too keen on the idea of keeping his folks long on a holiday weekend. But it is was obvious God was up to something. He stepped down from the platform to join Steve. As soon as he moved into the altar area, Kilpatrick noticed what seemed to be a strong gust of air swirling around the floor. The air moved about his legs like a river of water, making it difficult to move. He then heard a sound coming from somewhere in the room. It rumbled and roared like wind being blown across a microphone. He looked up toward the speakers clustered above his head, but the sound wasn't coming from there. It was coming from behind him.[11]

It sounded like a violent wind, and it rushed into the sanctuary from above the platform before spilling into the altar. Kilpatrick felt it flow right between his legs, forcing both his knees to buckle outward. It was an overwhelming experience.[12]

There was a man close by who noticed that his pastor was struggling to hold himself up. He went to him and helped Kilpatrick back to the platform, where he could address the people. Kilpatrick picked up the pulpit microphone and began to speak. What came out of his mouth, he didn't intend to say. It leaped out from the depths of his spirit.[13] In a loud voice he proclaimed, "I have never felt the power of God like I feel it right now... I am telling you this, there is power in this place... the glory of God... don't fear. Just receive it!"[14] John Kilpatrick was convinced that this was the outpouring the church had been praying for, and he wanted his people to get in.

The moment Pastor Kilpatrick spoke those words, the

heavens above the church seemed to open, and the Spirit of God descended into the room. Whole sections of people were swept right off their feet. From his vantage point on the stage, Kilpatrick saw people falling everywhere. He had never seen or personally experienced anything like it.[15] Even he found it difficult to hold himself up as the weight of God's glory surrounded him. He started to descend the steps once again, but instead collapsed hard to the floor. His head bounced on the marble floor of the stage.[16]

After the church had prayed one and a half years for it, revival had come to Brownsville Assembly of God. The service on Father's Day lasted through the afternoon. The sound of revival permeated the room. People were filled with joy and began to laugh and sing praises to the Lord. Others groaned and wept with the cries of repentance. Many just continued to lie on the floor or they sat in their seats in silence, enjoying the manifest presence of the Lord.[17]

Steve Hill was invited to stay as the services continued. Each night more people would come. Every night sinners filled the altar, repenting before the Lord. Hundreds were being saved.

A New Heart

When the Wards heard about the services happening that week, they weren't sure what to think. They went to church the following Sunday curious but cautious. Like so many, they were not too sure about what was happening at their church. This was very different from what they were used to. That night Amy's older sister, Alison, chose to respond to Steve's altar call. She was tired of living a double life. She had been dealing with depression and feeling pressured by the world around her. She prayed with Steve that night and quietly went home. The next day it was evident that something dramatic had taken place in Alison. Her mom noticed it right way. Everything about her eldest daughter was different. Her attitude and countenance had changed. There was a hunger for the Lord that hadn't existed the day before.[18]

The Wards didn't miss a service after that first night. Amy came along each night at the request of her mother and out of curiosity. She was still hard of heart, but the Lord was working on her. Each night she watched as her peers were visibly touched by the Spirit of God. By Thursday night Amy was finally open for the Lord to do something in her life. She went to the altar with Alison and waited for the evangelist to come pray for her. For more than two hours Steve would pass her by. Amy remained in the altar that entire time. She was used to getting her way, and tonight would be no different. She would make Steve pray for her, even if she was the last person there.[19]

Finally Steve came to Amy. When he prayed for her, something remarkable happened. He barely touched her forehead, yet she felt like something intense entered her body. Her strength melted away, and she crumbled to the floor. Amy lay there on the floor motionless and in complete peace. As she began to revive, she felt certain that this was a defining moment for her. All week long she had been discontent, trying to live two different lives. It was as if the Lord was asking her, "Will you take hold of Me or go back to your life of compromise?"[20]

Desperately desiring a total change, she prayed, "God, if You're going to do something, do it now!"[21] At that, she felt wave after wave of power begin to course through her from her neck to her waist. Every muscle in her body contracted tightly and then relaxed, causing her to convulse on the ground. The scene was so dramatic that it caught the attention of those around her. They knew Amy well enough to know that only God could be at work, as Amy would not fake such a thing.[22]

Amy could only describe it as a heart transplant. God was reaching deep within her, and He was removing that heart of stone and giving her a new heart of flesh. The encounter lasted three hours. When Amy got up, she was a different person. It was a total and complete transformation that was akin to Saul's on the road to Damascus.[23]

Steve Hill often said during the revival that God can do more in a single moment than man could accomplish in a lifetime. That was certainly true for Amy. There was no more going back to the compromise of the past. Everything was different now. As a reminder to herself and a testimony to those around her, she felt she had to change her name. Everyone knew Amy to be a rebellious girl. She was no longer that. She asked that people call her by her middle name, Elizabeth, from then on. Elizabeth means consecrated to the Lord, and that was exactly what she was.[24]

As the summer drew to a close, the crowds at Brownsville continued to grow. It was Friday, August 18, and the church was crowded. People were not only packed in the sanctuary, but also they were in the cafeteria and in the old sanctuary that sat across the street. Hundreds of people had come early that night. Some started lining up in front of the doors of the church at 6:00 a.m. just to ensure themselves a seat. It wasn't just church folk who stood in line. There were scores of sinners as well. They came in desperation, hoping to meet with God and find deliverance.

On Fridays the church always took time in the middle of the service to share testimonies from the revival. Amy's sister, Alison, was asked to share that night about the powerful manifestations she had experienced and to talk about how she was being used in intercessory prayer during the revival.

As the service transitioned, Pastor Kilpatrick took the stage and asked for Alison to come share her testimony about the revival. As she did, the Spirit of God came on her, causing her body to shake. It looked as if a strong electric current was flowing through her. Alison was a very slender girl with long, curly dark hair. Every time her head would shake, her long hair would move through the air like a tree stirred by a strong gust of wind. It was certainly an unusual sight for most in attendance, especially those new to the revival.[25]

Pastor Kilpatrick introduced Alison to the church as Amy's sister. Amy had testified weeks earlier; now it was her sister's opportunity. He then said when people see someone shaking as Alison was, they may make a snap judgment and question what is going on. He shared his background with Alison and her family. He wanted the people to know that what they were witnessing was not a work of the flesh. "God uses her when it comes time for the altar call...in intercession," he said. "You'll see her back there [in the sanctuary] under the power of the Holy Spirit interceding for lost souls. I know these girls. I know beyond any doubt that these girls are being moved on by the Holy Spirit."[26]

With that, he helped Alison to the pulpit. As she stepped behind the pulpit, she began to shake even more. It took a moment for her to steady her hand so she could share part of her testimony. She said, "All through high school and college, God...had a place in my heart, but He didn't really have a place in my life. I never thought that God had anything to offer other than just sitting at church. I'd never given Him a chance to do anything in my life. So I was constantly running after the world. I thought I had to have something that the world would give me. But when I heard what Steve preached, my eyes were opened....I was blinded by worldly things that I thought I had to have and worldly friends that I thought I had to have, and all it took to totally change my life was for me to listen and really hear what these men of God are trying to say, what God is trying to say. The Bible says, people have ears to hear but they don't hear...what God is trying to say to them. I listened that night, and God totally opened my eyes and He changed my whole life."[27]

She was referring to that second week of the revival when she and her sister were radically transformed. She then likened her former lukewarm life to the Laodicean church mentioned in Revelation. She said, "God says Himself He'd rather spit you out of His mouth than have you be lukewarm, because you're no good to anybody unless you're hot or cold." She then paused before she said, "So, I'm hot now!"[28]

At that, the entire place erupted in loud applause and praise. Pastor Kilpatrick took this as an opportunity to address the manifestation she was currently exhibiting. He knew people would have doubts and even criticize the revival based on these manifestations. This was a chance to give these strange sights some context. He asked her, "Whenever this is on you, Alison, you don't have pain, do you?"[29]

"No, it's not painful at all," she said.[30] There was gentleness in her answer. It was obvious she cherished this manifestation as a gift, not a burden.

The pastor then asked Alison to try to describe what she was feeling. Alison said, "Right now, I think the glory of God is so strong up here, my body just can't really take it....But there's other times when I come into God's presence, I don't move at all. But inside me, it's like there are just waves of God inside of me. Then there [are] other times when I'm interceding, and it's not painful to my body, but it's painful to my heart."[31]

The emotion in Alison's voice now showed. She felt every word she was saying. "Because I know that God loves people so much"—she paused, as if the next words were particularly hard to say—"and He's...He's...He is in a hurry!"[32]

When Alison said, "He's in a hurry," it was like a sudden awareness of impending judgment moved into the church. Even Pastor Kilpatrick felt it. It was as if the weight of those words hit him deep in his own spirit like a hard punch to the gut, and he actually grabbed his stomach. He wasn't the only one. In one moment that same realization came upon the congregation, not only those in the sanctuary but also the overflow crowds who were watching the service in the cafeteria and the chapel. Everyone seemed to be feeling exactly what Alison was feeling.[33]

Alison continued, "He wants...He wants everyone. There is not much...not much more time! He aches and He grieves for your spirit! He grieves for you!"[34]

Alison could no longer stand on her feet. She tried to steady herself onto the pulpit but couldn't hold herself up. Pastor Kilpatrick collapsed to his knees as well. He grabbed the side of the pulpit with his right arm in an attempt to hold himself up but couldn't.

An avalanche of God's holy presence rushed throughout the entire campus, and a divine urgency gripped everyone in the room. A collective groan was released across the campus, and the sound of weeping and wailing filled the house. Across the street the youth pastor, Richard Crisco, was watching over the overflow crowd that had gathered in the chapel. When Alison said, "He is in a hurry," he said it felt as if the air was instantly let out of the room, catching everyone by surprise. It hit Richard so hard he couldn't even stay in the room. He ran for the back door and went outside to catch his breath. When he returned to the chapel minutes later, the scene was something to behold. Sinners who had been brought by friends had fallen from their seats and were now in a fetal position, wailing at the top of their lungs, crying out for mercy. He watched as many were picked up by their loved ones and brought to the steps of the altar and deposited before the Lord.[35]

That night, in both the sanctuary and the overflow rooms, multitudes of people ran to the altar to find mercy at the feet of Jesus. They fell on their knees and cried out to the Lord in repentance while everyone else groaned in intercession. That night God wanted everyone to experience that same spirit of intercession that had gripped Alison, and thousands did.

GOD IS STILL IN A HURRY!

Of the thousands of services that took place at Brownsville, this night was certainly one of the most known. The testimonies of Amy Elizabeth and Alison Ward were later edited together and made available on a single thirty-minute videotape. Thousands of copies were distributed in the months following and began to circulate across the country and then around the world. Copies of copies were made, and the video was passed hand to hand, house to house, and church to church. It is highly possible that this was the world's first viral video, passed along without the aid of the Internet. For millions around the world, the testimonies of Elizabeth and Alison Ward became their first exposure to the revival in Brownsville.

Each time the video was played in homes, churches, or conferences across the nation, the effect was similar to that night. Those who saw it felt the urgency of the moment. Pastors played it for their churches, and people would spontaneously run to the altar. Others would watch it in their homes and fall to their knees before their television sets. Millions of people were first exposed to the fires of Pensacola thanks to the videotape of the Wards' testimonies. It wasn't long before churches began to charter buses and families rearranged vacations so they could visit the revival in Pensacola. The conservative estimate is that nearly four million people visited the revival during its five years, and more than one hundred fifty thousand people gave their lives to Jesus at the altar.[36] The Brownsville revival is noted as the longest-running, largest-attended revival in American history.[37]

I for one will never forget the first time I saw the video. It was spring break of 1996, and I was in the second semester of my freshman year of college. I had been invited to attend a youth conference in Summerville, South Carolina, and I decided to go. Honestly, I went to Summerville to be close to friends and the beach, not go to church. Much like Amy Ward, I too was a calloused and rebellious young man. Though I had grown up in church and knew things about God, I didn't really know Him. Church was just something I did; I refused to let it define my life.

At the conference an evangelist who had been to the revival in Pensacola spoke. I don't remember his name or his message, but I do remember him sharing the video of Amy and Alison Ward. It shook the lives of the hundreds of teenagers in the church that morning, most of whom could identify with Amy's testimony. When Alison shared, you could feel the shift in the room. The same divine sense of urgency gripped us all.

The evangelist wasted no time and gave the altar call as soon as the video was over. Everyone in the room ran down to the front of the church at once—everyone but me. I stood in the very back of the church for another forty-five minutes with both hands gripping the back of the seat in front of me. I was hanging on, hoping the altar call would come to a close and I could relax. Finally the appeal came to an end, and I sat down. I fought so hard for so long, and it looked like I might escape that morning without surrendering to Christ. Thankfully the evangelist took one more opportunity. He invited the few remaining in their seats to come to the altar if they wanted to get closer to the Lord.

To this day I don't know why I sprung up and walked down to the altar, but I'm glad I did. Perhaps it was the fact that after my fighting so hard, the Holy Spirit saw a moment when my guard was down. He gently tugged and I responded. I went to the altar and lifted my hands to the Lord. I was in a posture of surrender, and the Lord heard my prayer.

What happened next I didn't expect. I felt the strength leave my body, and I could no longer stand up. I fell to ground and landed hard on my back. I had seen this before but had never experienced it. I had even made fun of it in the past, and now here I was lying on the ground unable to move. I tried to wrap my mind around what was taking place, but I couldn't. That was when the Lord began speaking to me about the call on my life that I had been running from. That morning He awakened in me a burden for my generation and an urgency for the hour in which I live. I have no idea how long I was on the ground, but I do know that when I got up, everything was different and has been ever since. That was the power of what God did through Brownsville. It didn't just affect those in Pensacola. That fire reached around the world.

Though it was decades ago when Alison reminded the church that God is in a hurry, that truth is even more relevant today than it was the night she spoke it. God has not slowed down, nor has He let up. He has never been in retreat. He has been forcefully advancing to this very day as His eternal clock continues to wind down. The day of His return is at hand. My friend, God is still in a hurry!

Jesus said, "I am coming quickly. Hold firmly what you have, so that no one may take your crown" (Rev. 3:11). Today the soon return of Christ has become a forgotten message. Where is the urgency we once had? Alison Ward's testimony in 1995 came as a much-needed wake-up call to the church. God's people were once again reminded of the shortness of the days in which we live and became convinced of the imminent return of Christ. Sadly that urgency faded, and the church has been lulled back to sleep.

Paul wrote, "The day of the Lord so cometh as a thief in the night" (1 Thess. 5:2, KJV). A thief does not arrive in the light of day when you are at home and awake. He comes in the middle of the night when you are fast asleep. He comes when you least expect him.

Revival always brings with it a sense of urgency. It sets eternity in view of both the sinner and saint, and the brevity of life becomes painfully evident to both.

One of the surest signs of Christ's soon return is a church that is fast asleep. Jesus made this clear: "Concerning that day and hour no one knows, not even the angels of heaven, but My Father only. As were the days of Noah, so will be the coming of the Son of Man. For as in the days before the flood, they were eating and drinking, marrying and giving in marriage, until the day Noah entered the ark, and did not know until the flood came and took them all away, so will be the coming of the Son of Man. Two will be in the field; one will be taken, and the other left. Two women will be grinding at the mill; one will be taken, and the other left. Watch therefore, for you do not know what hour your Lord will come. But know this, that if the owner of the house had known what hour the thief would come, he would have watched and not have let his house be broken into. Therefore you also must be ready, for in an hour when you least expect, the Son of Man is coming" (Matt. 24:36–44).

I find it interesting that many would-be prophets prophesy great trials and tribulations to accompany the days preceding Christ's return. They trumpet doomsday scenarios to gin up donations and sell products. I don't believe the days before Christ's return will be so dire. Jesus said that a sleeping church would be the sign of His return. It will be like in the days of Noah. The day before the Flood people were eating, drinking, and partying as if they had all the time in the world. They weren't living in fear. They weren't experiencing desperate times. They had only hours left, yet they lived as if they had all the time in the world. A man of God had cautioned them to repent, but they scoffed at the prophet and continued in their ways. In Matthew 24 Christ warns His disciples not to be lulled into a false sense of security. He said, "Be ready, for in an hour when you least expect it, I am coming!"

Awake! Awake, O sleeper! This could be the very hour of His return. He is in a hurry, and there is not much more time left! If ever there has been a season when a sense of urgency is needed, it is now. Revival always brings with it a sense of urgency. It sets eternity in view of both the sinner and saint, and the brevity of life becomes painfully evident to both. The sinner who is lost and away from God becomes convinced that today is the only day of salvation. Without that urgency, the person will always delay another day, hoping to get one more night of compromise in before he surrenders. However, when a person senses the urgency of the hour, he realizes that tomorrow is promised to no one. He falls at Jesus's feet, pleading for mercy. We see this in every move of God and will see it in the next! This is why deep cries of repentance could be heard night after night at the altars at Brownsville. People understood that God was in a hurry.

Likewise, when the saint realizes the urgency of the hour, he is suddenly motivated to engage in the work of the kingdom. During the Brownsville Revival a school was launched for this very purpose. By 1999 there were fourteen hundred students being trained and equipped to take the gospel around the world. Decades later these men and women are serving in churches and ministries here in the United States and throughout the nations.

As believers we must live with our eyes upon the horizon and our hands upon the harvest. You and I have only this life to live and this life to give. We can spend it any way we choose, but we can spend it only once. After it's spent, it is gone. We don't get to try again. Every conversation and every opportunity you have today is a chance to see the kingdom of God become manifest in someone else's life. When there is no urgency, we treat those moments as if we will get another. However, when the urgency is there, we do whatever it takes to make the most of each moment. God is still in a hurry!

Where is the urgency? Jesus said, "I am coming quickly" (Rev. 3:11). When the urgency is lost, we live for the present day. We become consumed with things that fade and ultimately do not matter. However, when our eyes are set upon eternity, we see the finish line. With your eyes properly fixed, everything comes into proper focus. There is no time to waste. We must fight hard, run hard, and hold to our faith, knowing that when we cross the finish line, Christ is waiting to reward us accordingly.

When the urgency is lost, all is lost, but when that urgency is found, the harder we fight. Alison reminded the church that God is in a hurry. God used that cry from the depths of her being to help spread revival far and wide. It's time we hear that cry once again. There is not a moment to waste because God is still in a hurry!

Speaking of Brownsville, Steve Hill once said, "That is what God did; it's not what He is doing." Steve lived convinced that the greatest move of God was not behind us but before us. I believe that to be true. It has to be true. Brownsville was an amazing period for millions of people, but it is history. It now reminds us of what God can do if we will once again sense an urgency in this hour and contend for another move of God. Our nation and world are in need of a greater awakening! It is time to wake up to the urgency of the hour in which we live and pray like never before that God would do it again. "He who testifies to these things says, 'Surely I am coming quickly.' Amen. Even so, come, Lord Jesus!" (Rev. 22:20, NKJV).

It is high time for women to let their lights shine; to bring out their talents that have been hidden away rusting, and use them for the glory of God, and do with their might what their hands find to do, trusting God for strength, who has said, "I will never leave you."[1]

—Maria Woodworth-Etter

Chapter 11

GOD IS NO RESPECTER
OF PERSONS

Our Daughters Also Shall Prophesy

*And it shall come to pass afterward that I
will pour out My Spirit on all flesh; your sons
and your daughters shall prophesy...*

—Joel 2:28, NKJV

1880, New Lisbon, Ohio

THE VISION CAME suddenly, startling the thirty-five-year-old housewife out of her slumber. There at her bedside stood Jesus. His face shone with heavenly brilliance, and the room was filled with His glory. Like Isaiah, Maria Woodworth-Etter found herself completely undone in the presence of the Lord. The Lord had not come this night to comfort but to confront His daughter. There was a sternness to His countenance and a boldness in His voice as He asked, "What are you doing on earth?"

His words came as a challenge to her current state of complacency. Woodworth-Etter knew she was called to preach. She had felt it ever since she was saved at the age of thirteen. Back then America was experiencing its Second Great Awakening, and Maria saw it firsthand. Her family was

196 TRAIL of FIRE

attending a large revival meeting, and she responded to the altar call. That night the evangelist took a great interest in the young girl and prayed over her that she would become a shining light to the world. Perhaps he had seen in her what the Lord was now seeking to reignite.

It had been more than twenty-two years since, and she had done nothing to fulfill that call. She had plenty of excuses. The early death of her father had prevented her from getting an education. With few choices she settled down with a farmer who had little interest in ministry. He wanted a simple housewife. The couple suffered through their own share of tragedy. Their farm was a failure. Her physical health was a continual issue, and illness claimed the lives of five of their six children. There was no arguing that the road behind them had been tough. Life had handed her one setback after the next, making ministry an unscalable mountain. However, the greatest excuse Woodworth-Etter had was that she wasn't a man.

She thought her season for ministry had passed; the Lord thought otherwise. This night the Lord Himself was directly confronting her doubts. He wanted to know what she was here on earth to do.

"Lord, I am going to work in Thy vineyard," she answered.

"When?" He asked.

"When I get prepared for the work," she said.

Jesus pressed further, "Don't you know that while you are getting ready, souls are perishing? Go now, and I will be with you."

"I don't know what to say!" Woodworth-Etter rebutted.

His answer remained the same: "Go now, and I will be with you."

"I don't know where to go," she responded.

Once again He said: "Go now, and I will be with you."[2]

She reached for yet another excuse. "I want to study the Bible. I don't understand it enough."

The Lord directed her attention toward the wall where His Word appeared as if it was projected upon a screen. All of Scripture was opened before her verse by verse. A verse was then lifted from the text. It stood out with raised letters, and the glory of God began to shine out from it. She looked intently upon the scripture and immediately understood it. That night Woodworth-Etter received a greater revelation of the Word than years of careful study could have provided.

Once again the Lord reminded His handmaiden, "Go now, and I will be with you."

Woodworth-Etter chose to start there in her own home. She invited her neighbors over, most of whom were relatives. The budding minister wasn't sure what to say that night. She simply waited for the Lord to give her a verse; from there she shared whatever the Lord dropped within her spirit. The words came to her faster than she could think. Immediately their home was filled with the presence of the Lord, and the handful who had gathered began to weep. Next to Woodworth-Etter sat her sister-in-law. She became so gripped by conviction that she couldn't control herself. She jumped up from her seat and bolted from the home with her hand over her mouth and tears streaming from her eyes.[3]

It was obvious that the hand of the Lord was on this woman, and word of her meetings began to spread. Invitations began to come from multiple churches despite the fact that she was a woman. The crowds continued to grow with each meeting. Woodworth-Etter was quickly proving the call on her life and becoming known as a powerful revivalist gifted at sparking awakening within churches.

She had been preaching only a few months when an invitation came from an old church that was located in a town just six miles from her home. She knew the town well. Locally it was referred to as "the Devil's Den." It was a place marked by infidelity, drunkenness, and skepticism. The lone church was barely attended and had never recorded a single salvation.

Woodworth-Etter was reluctant to consider the invitation. Some of the best ministers had labored there in vain. All of their attempts to revive the church and town had failed. Every one of them ran out in disgust. They were convinced this hellish town had no hope. Woodworth-Etter felt unprepared for so great a task, yet the Lord's words remained fixed in her mind. He said, "Go now, and I'll be with you." She was about to discover exactly what the Lord meant.

When Woodworth-Etter arrived in town, she found it to be as unwelcoming as she expected. It was immediately apparent that she would be alone in her work. She had to do all the promotion and preparation for the meetings. Time and again she was warned that no one would show up at her religious meetings. However, that first night there was a crowd at the old church, even if most had simply come out of curiosity. They were looking forward to seeing the woman preacher run out of town or, even better, too scared to show her face.

Woodworth-Etter had to conduct the entire meeting alone. She opened with prayer then led the congregation in worship. She was the only one singing. She then turned to the Word and began to preach as the Spirit led. The service ended with not a single response. The same was true for the second and third night as well. It seemed as if she might be joining that long list of failed preachers.

Woodworth-Etter wouldn't give up so easily. She was emboldened by another encounter she had at the beginning of her ministry. She had seen a vision of angels descending from heaven. They came like an army until she was completely surrounded. She was then lifted up into the air and carried miles away and sat in the midst of a vast field of wheat. It spread as far as her eye could see and seemed to have no end. An intense burden for the lost consumed her, and she was immediately filled with great zeal. She began to boldly proclaim the Word of the Lord, and as she did, the wheat began to fall down all around her. That vision became her driving force to finish what the Lord had commissioned her to do. She knew she had no choice. She must preach.[4]

That burden for the lost weighed heavily on her. She knew she had been brought to the Devil's Den and was convinced that even the hardest of sinners could be converted. She knew exactly what she must do. She called a prayer meeting to take place that following afternoon. She was informed that no one would come to a day meeting. However, her mind was made up. She rebuked the scoffers, saying if no one else came, she would go and pray for God to pour out His power upon the people. She was now convinced that God was ready to shake the foundation of the city and awaken the dry bones in the Devil's Den. That afternoon she began to intercede and allowed the burden to fully take hold of her, and there in her anguish she laid hold of the Lord.

That night her prayers were answered, and revival was birthed in the heart of the city. The hand of the Lord came upon her, and she spoke with great passion and authority. A man entered the meeting completely drunk. He came to disrupt things, but as she preached, he was sobered up. He fell before the Lord in true brokenness and was radically saved. He wasn't alone—the hardest and vilest of sinners found the grace of God there in the Devil's Den. Her words quickly humbled the crowd. Grown men turned pale and began to shake and tremble in their seats under the conviction of the Lord. They came to the Lord in tears. This woman of God had accomplished what so many men had failed to do.

News about the revival in Devil's Den began to spread like fire. Crowds began to turn out from miles around to witness this miracle. The Lord provided Woodworth-Etter with all the help she needed for the revival. There were singers and musicians to help with worship, teachers for Bible studies, and leaders for the prayer meetings. Within days the old church had reached its capacity. The windows and doors had to be opened so people could listen in from outside.

Woodworth-Etter was there for two weeks. During that time she arranged a weekly Sabbath service along with a Sunday school that boasted 150 students. The superintendent for the Sunday school was the former drunk who had been saved just two weeks earlier! Local ministers were recruited to rotate through the church to keep the pulpit filled. She was only a few months into her ministry and already she had planted a church! There was no questioning that the Lord was using this woman of God.[5]

Fast-forward thirty-two years. Since the revival in the Devil's Den, the road in ministry had certainly been rough for Woodworth-Etter, but it was also rewarding. It was 1912, and she was now a national phenomenon and a prominent voice in the Pentecostal movement. Remarkable signs, wonders, and miracles followed her ministry, and several times she had ministered to more than twenty thousand at a time. Maria Woodworth-Etter had proven that a woman could take a central role in revival.

Pastor Fred Bosworth had invited Woodworth-Etter to participate in an ongoing Pentecostal revival that had been taking place over the last seventeen months in Dallas, Texas.[6] There was great anticipation of her arrival, as thousands had already come to receive the Pentecostal blessing.

The revival had been meeting under a large tent in east Dallas next to the state fairgrounds. The night Woodworth-Etter arrived, there were five thousand people packed under and around the tent. They had come by train and wagon, some from as far away as Canada. A large number were sick and disabled. They were carried in on cots and entered in wheel-chairs. For many it was a disturbing scene.

Woodworth-Etter had grown over the years in her anointing. Though she was a tiny woman, she was a spiritual giant. As she spoke that night, the power of God descended upon the crowd. Hundreds of men and women fell to the ground at one time. Some would lie there for hours, often having visions of heaven or hell.

As the meeting progressed, Woodworth-Etter called for those sick in body to come forward. One of the first to approach was a backslidden man who had come from sev-eral hundred miles away. He had recently fallen and broken three ribs. The bones had turned into his lungs, and he arrived that night in incredible pain. Woodworth-Etter laid her hands on the man's chest, and he flinched from the dis-comfort. Then, to the surprise of the man and the audience, the pain immediately left. He felt and heard his ribs snap back into place. He was overwhelmed and surrendered his life to Jesus right there. He then stood before the crowd tes-tifying to the miracle, beating the side of his body with a closed fist to prove he was completely healed.[7]

Also in the meeting was a woman who arrived on a gurney. She was suffering severely from cancer in her stomach as well as tuberculosis. She was nothing but skin and bones with little life left in her. The best doctors in Dallas had given up on her. They sent her home to die. It wasn't advisable for her to be taken from her home, yet she was willing to risk it. Her family thought she might pass that night. They patiently waited for the evangelist to come pray for her. Pastor Fred Bosworth watched in amazement as Woodworth-Etter laid hands on the woman. It took only a few moments for life to return to her body. She stood up from her gurney instantly healed of both conditions. She began shouting and praising the Lord, along with all those in attendance. The woman didn't miss a meeting after that night and often testified during the revival. Woodworth-Etter ended up staying in Dallas for seven months. It was one of her greatest revival meetings.[8]

THE HEROINES OF REVIVAL

The trail of fire demonstrates that God is no respecter of persons with regard to who He will use to fan the flames of revival. History has certainly focused heavily on the men who shook their nation, but look closer. Oftentimes at the core of that fire you will find a woman who played a significant role.

For instance, it was Susanna Wesley who gave her son the spiritual foundation that led John Wesley to spark a national awakening in England. It could be said that Wesley's Methodism was first developed and proven in the home of Susanna Wesley. Susanna reached John before John reached the world. Today's Methodist Church owes as much to her as it does to him.

> God can and will use anyone—male or female, young or old, regardless of race. Anyone can be a candidate to be used in the next great move of God. The only requirement is a willingness to go.

Did you notice that it was a young Dutch woman named Miss Van Blerk who sparked the great move of God in South Africa? Burdened for the neglected African people, she was the first to see something her own minister had missed. Revival came as an answer to her intercession.

Likewise the evangelist Duncan Campbell became the beneficiary of the answered prayer of two elderly sisters, Peggy and Christine Smith. They were the ones who first carried the burden. They prayed until that revival became a reality.

Though Steve Hill will be remembered as the preacher of the Brownsville Revival, for millions of people their first exposure to that move of God was through the testimonies of Alison and Amy Ward. It is possible that Alison's testimony may have brought the spirit of revival to more people than any person in history.

God can and will use anyone—male or female, young or old, regardless of race. Anyone can be a candidate to be used in the next great move of God. The only requirement is a willingness to go. Maria Woodworth-Etter discovered this, and it became the secret to her success. She simply had faith in God's Word. He said, "And it shall come to pass afterward, that I will pour out My Spirit on all flesh; your sons and your daughters shall prophesy" (Joel 2:28, NKJV). She saw what was hidden in plain sight. God didn't say, "Your sons shall prophesy," He said, "Your sons and your daughters shall prophesy." Clearly it is God's will to use *all flesh*. He never intended for the sons to have a monopoly on ministry.

When the Spirit of God was poured out on the Day of Pentecost, it fell upon 120 believers. There were both men and women present that day. Afterward Peter stood before thousands of onlookers and preached the first Pentecostal message. He said this was what Joel had prophesied. God was beginning to pour out His Spirit on His sons and daughters. The promise was available to anyone and everyone who would call upon His name. (See Acts 2:16–39.)

From that day on women have played a vital role in the church. Priscilla, along with her husband, Aquila, traveled with Paul helping to spread the gospel. They were Jews who had been banished from Rome. They first met Paul in Corinth and became believers. Later Paul left them to help the church at Ephesus. It is clear Priscilla was a tremendous blessing. (See Acts 18:2, 26; Romans 16:3–5, 16).

Phoebe is another woman mentioned with honor in the New Testament. The Apostle Paul commends her to the church in Rome. He asked that she be welcomed as an elder and that she be given whatever assistance she needed (Rom. 16:1–2). Euodia and Syntyche were two women in Philippi whom Paul commended alongside Clement as co-laborers in the gospel (Phil. 4:2–3). Paul's numerous mentions of his female coworkers demonstrate he was proponent, not an opponent, of women in ministry. He wrote that in the eyes of Christ, "There is neither Jew nor Greek, there is neither slave nor free, and there is neither male nor female, for you are all one in Christ Jesus" (Gal. 3:28).

Maria Woodworth-Etter was another minister to continue a rich heritage of women who played an important role in spreading the gospel. She moved in true apostolic signs and wonders and is as important to the modern Pentecostal movement as is William Seymour. Woodworth-Etter defied the cultural bias that had existed for centuries and became the first lady of modern revival. She showed that God can use anyone who simply trusts Him. She opened wide the eyes of many to the idea that a woman could be used in a great move of God, and she pioneered the way for those who would come after her.

Aimee Semple McPherson followed Woodworth-Etter as an evangelist who operated in great signs and wonders as well. McPherson's meetings attracted more than ten thousand. She built a five-thousand-seat church in Los Angles and filled it three times a day. She went on to found the International Church of the Foursquare Gospel and the world's first Christian radio station.[9] Following in McPherson's steps was Kathryn Kuhlman. Like Woodworth-Etter and McPherson,

Kuhlman's ministry was marked by miracles. She developed a worldwide media audience through her television broadcast, which at one time was the longest running broadcast in the CBS studios' history.[10]

The influence of such women of God has had a profound effect on the church in the last century. I often think about my own grandmother, Celeste Kimball, who was baptized in the Holy Spirit while studying the Book of Acts in a small rural Baptist church outside Portland, Maine. She was a mother of seven and separated from an abusive husband. The fire that burned in her could not be stilled or silenced. Following the example of these heroines of revival, she moved south to help start a missionary training school in the foothills of South Carolina. Through the years I have been pleasantly surprised to discover how far around the world her influence extended. She's reached nations because she followed the Lord's call to go.

At this moment God is using women greatly for the cause of Christ all over the world. The only wall that stands between you and your call is belief. The Lord came to Maria Woodworth-Etter at her bedside and confronted her complacency. That night He removed her excuses and promised her that if she would go, He would be with her. The same is true for each of us. Woodworth-Etter said, "God is calling the Marys and the Marthas today all over our land to work in various places in the vineyard of the Lord; God grant that they may respond and say, 'Lord, here am I; send me.'"[11]

Who knows? Perhaps the next great move of God will come through a great woman of God. As Maria Woodworth-Etter wrote, "God is promising great blessings and power to qualify His handmaidens for the last great harvest just before the notable Day of the Lord comes...the Lord says women shall prophesy."[12]

*According to the weight of the burden that grieves
you is the cry to God that comes from you.*[1]

—Joseph Caryl, 1673

Conclusion

THE TRAIL OF FIRE CONTINUES

I WAS DOWNSTAIRS IN my office working on the very first story in the book you now hold in your hand. I had immersed myself in the writings of Jonathan Edwards and the accounts of America's First Great Awakening. As I wrote about the revival in Enfield, my spirit was stirred. Tears began to flow from my eyes as I was gripped with an intense, burning burden for revival. Oh, how far this nation has slipped from its foundations! There are so few churches that would be comfortable with Edwards's kind of preaching in their pulpits. It is a shame to say he would be unwelcome in our day. This reality grieves me. Edwards is a celebrated minister, yet his message to the church is forgotten. Over and over I kept praying, "God, give us a *greater* awakening!"

It was at that moment my wife walked in with her phone in hand. "You've got to see this," she said. There on her phone was a picture of a two-hundred-year-old-church pew from the First Church of Christ in New London, Connecticut. Because I was doing research on Edwards, I already knew the name of the church and some of its history. The First Church of Christ had hosted some of the greatest men of God from America's First Great Awakening. Generals such as George Whitefield, David Brainerd, and even Jonathan Edwards graced its pulpit. That bench was a witness to the very history I was writing about, and it was being offered for sale by the church that currently owns the building.

I can only imagine all the messages that pew heard over the years. I can picture the bench packed with people who came to hear Whitefield or Edwards preach. I imagine some of them gripping the back of the pew with firmly clasped hands, digging their nails into the wood as they fell under the conviction of the Holy Spirit. I envision others falling from the bench and lying prostrate on the ground beneath the pew, having been struck by the sword of the Lord.

This was a remarkable piece, and here it was in front of me as I was literally writing about the history it was part of. I heard the words of Leonard Ravenhill resounding in my mind, "The opportunity of a lifetime must be seized within the lifetime of the opportunity."[2] I didn't waste any time. Within the hour I was speaking to the pastor at the church and had secured the pew. It now sits in my office. Steve Hill would be jealous, as this is the very type of thing he loved to put in his own office.

I don't think this was a coincidence. Yes, I understand there's nothing sacred about this piece of furniture. Yet I can't escape its significance. You see, the desk I was using to write this book has significance as well. Steve Hill gave it to me before he passed away. It is a beautiful old antique English desk that he had purchased during the Brownsville Revival for his own office. Behind that desk Steve wrote messages such as "White Cane Religion," "The God Mockers," "Check the Tree," and "Arrows of the Lord." Only heaven knows how many hours of study and prayer Steve invested before the Lord upon that desk.

Now both of these historic pieces from America's First Great Awakening and its last great revival sit in my office. The pew and the desk are both intrinsically connected to the beginning and end of the book you're reading. Personally they remind me that I myself am connected to a trail of fire that has burned through history. What an honor to have been preceded by such a great cloud of witnesses, and how humbling it is to recognize the awesome responsibility of the road that lies ahead. I am encouraged to further throw off every weight and run the race that is marked out for me.

You realize that you are connected to this trail of fire as well, don't you? My friend, I am bold enough to believe there is a reason this book is in your hands. These stories are not just history. They are part of *your* history. You did not arrive at this moment by accident. You were preceded by a man or woman of God who brought the unquenchable fire of the gospel to you. The same fire that first burned on the Day of Pentecost has been passed down over the last two thousand years, and now it rests in your hands. What happens next is up to you! Will you let it fully consume you, or will you be content to remain in your current state of comfort?

As you read through the trail of fire, surely your spirit was stirred—and I hope something was awakened within you! Did the story of Edwards's meeting in Enfield bring eternity closer into view? Did reading the story of Cane Ridge ignite an expectancy within your spirit? Those were spiritually dry days in America, yet God used the dry brush to start a fire. If He did it before, I can expect that He will do it again.

How about the sound of revival that was heard across The Cape Colony in South Africa? Did it stir you to a place of prayer? That is the only way revival comes. Did Charles Finney's revival in Antwerp cause you to look upon the fallowed ground of your own heart and repent before the Lord? Surely you wanted to pray with Evan Roberts, "Lord, bend me," as you read about the revival in Wales. Maybe now you better understood the unique power of sacrifice as you read about the revival in Korea.

Did reading about the Azusa Street Revival show you the necessity of unity in the body of Christ? God is not looking for another church but one church! My all-time favorite story, the one about Hebrides, reminds us to take up the burden of the Lord and believe an entire land can be saved. Last, how can you read about Brownsville and not sense the urgency of the hour in which we live? I pray these stories were like wind blown upon smoldering embers. I pray they ignited a burning burden within you for revival.

There is a lot of talk about revival these days. It seems many are interested in revival, yet few are truly burdened for revival. Interest isn't enough. Revival doesn't come because we were interested in it; it comes because someone was burdened for it. Interest speaks to a fascination or curiosity, but a burden speaks to an insatiable desire. A man or woman with a burden will lay everything down, pray through the night, and not relent until heaven answers. That is the type of cry that gets heaven's attention. I pray such a thing is being awakened in you. Steve Hill once told me about a time when he and Jeri were at home between their missions assignments. This was before the revival broke out in Pensacola. They had moved to Lindell, Texas, to be closer to his mentor, Leonard Ravenhill. For Steve, it was a time marked by a particular heaviness. No matter how hard he prayed, he couldn't shake the burden he felt growing deep within his spirit. He asked his mentor to pray that the Lord would remove it from him. Ravenhill's response was classic. He said, "Why should I ask God to lift this from you when I've been praying that He would put it on you?"

The Puritan writer Joseph Caryl said, "According to the weight of the burden that grieves you, is the cry to God that comes from you."[3] We don't need to wonder what kind of burden a person is under. We need only to listen to the prayers the person offers, for out of the abundance of the heart the mouth speaks (Luke 6:45).

What cry is coming from you? Remember, revival comes

as a response. It is heaven's answer to the persistent and passionate cries of God's holy people. In order for heaven to respond, there must first be a request. No doubt we see the need, but necessity in itself does not bring the answer. In true humility and contrition we must position ourselves before the Lord and seek His face.

Revival doesn't come because we were interested in it; it comes because someone was burdened for it. What are you crying out to the Lord for? Is it possible that as you've read through these stories you have at times found yourself stirred to pray? Don't discount that stirring! Something has been awakened in you.

This trail of fire has come to you, and now is the time it must burn through you. Each of these stories is simply a reminder that God can use anyone and everyone. He can use you! Do you long to see God pour out His spirit in your life, your family, your community, or your nation? Let that be the cry that comes from you.

> Revival doesn't come because we were interested in it; it comes because someone was burdened for it.

Paul wrote to his young protégé, Timothy, "Stir up the gift of God which is in you through the laying on of my hands. For God has not given us a spirit of fear but of power and of love and of a sound mind" (2 Tim. 1:6–7, NKJV). Do you see it? Do you now realize how you are connected to this continuing trail of fire? I encourage you: do not let the fire go out on your watch. Fan it to flame and let it fully consume you. Even if that cry is currently a whisper, fan it any way. Soon it will erupt from you like a violent shout to the Lord, and heaven will respond. The next great move of God must start somewhere. Why not let the trail of fire continue through you?

NOTES

INTRODUCTION—A FIRE BURNS

1. Leonard Ravenhill, *Why Revival Tarries* (Minneapolis, MN: Bethany House, 1979), 37.
2. Ibid.
3. Ibid., 39.

CHAPTER 1—STAMP ETERNITY ON MY EYES

1. Jonathan Edwards, *Sinners in the Hands of an Angry God* (Boston: T. Lumisden and J. Robertson, 1745), 15.
2. Leonard Ravenhill, "Your Day in Court," Ravenhill.org, accessed February 8, 2016, http://www.ravenhill.org/dayincourt.htm.
3. Thomas Kidd, *The Great Awakening* (New Haven, CT: Yale University Press, 2007), 106.
4. Ravenhill, "Your Day in Court."
5. David Jeremiah, *Jesus' Final Warning* (Nashville: Thomas Nelson, 1999), 162.
6. George M. Marsden, *Jonathan Edwards: A Life* (New Haven, CT: Yale University Press, 2003), 133.
7. Jonathan Edwards, *Letters and Personal Writings*, ed. George S. Claghorn (New Haven, CT: Yale University Press, 1998).
8. Stephen Williams, *Diary of Reverend Stephen Williams*, vol. 3 (Longmeadow, MA: Works Progress Administration, 1930), 374.
9. Enfield Historical Society, "Jonathan Edwards," accessed February 8, 2016, http://www.enfieldhistoricalsociety.org/EHSedwards.html.
10. Kidd, *The Great Awakening*, 101–106.
11. Michael K. Foster, Jack Campisi, and Marianne Mithun, eds., *Extending the Rafters: Interdisciplinary Approaches to Iroquoian Studies* (Albany, NY: State University of New York Press, 1984), 52.
12. Leonard Ravenhill, "Jonathan Edwards," Ravenhill.org, accessed February 8, 2016, http://www.ravenhill.org/edwards.htm.
13. Ibid.
14. Edwards, *Sinners in the Hands of an Angry God*, 15–16.
15. Ravenhill, "Jonathan Edwards."
16. Edwards, *Sinners in the Hands of an Angry God*, 16.
17. Ibid.
18. Williams, *Diary of Reverend Stephen Williams*, vol. 3, 375.
19. Edwards, *Sinners in the Hands of an Angry God*, 16–17.

20. Williams, *Diary of Reverend Stephen Williams*, vol. 3, 375.

21. Ravenhill, "Jonathan Edwards."

22. Williams, *Diary of Reverend Stephen Williams*, vol. 3, 375.

23. Marsden, *Jonathan Edwards: A Life*, Kindle edition, Kindle locations 3108–3114.

24. Stephen Hill, *Daily Awakenings* (Ventura, CA: Regal Books, 1999), 373.

25. Ravenhill, "Your Day in Court."

26. Ibid.

27. Micah Fries, Stephen Rummage, and Robby Gallaty, *Christ-Centered Exposition: Exalting Jesus in Zephaniah, Haggai, Zechariah, and Malachi* (Nashville: Holman Reference, 2015), 245.

28. Edwards, *Sinners in the Hands of an Angry God*, 15–16.

29. Leonard Ravenhill, "The Judgment Seat of Christ," accessed February 8, 2016, http://www.ravenhill.org/judgment.htm.

CHAPTER 2—FIRE ON THE FRONTIER

1. Barton Stone, *The Biography of Eld. Barton Warren Stone* (Cincinnati, OH: J. A. & U .P. James, 1847), 37.

2. Ibid.

3. D. Newell Williams, *Barton Stone: A Spiritual Biography* (St. Louis, Mo: Chalice Press, 2000), 58.

4. Stone, *The Biography of Eld. Barton Warren Stone*, 29

5. Ibid., 34.

6. Mark Galli, "Revival at Cane Ridge," Christian History Institute, accessed February 8, 2016, https://www.christianhistoryinstitute .org/magazine/article/revival-at-cane-ridge/.

7. Jeanine and Berkeley Scott, *Images of America: Paris and Bourbon County* (Charleston, SC: Arcadia Publishing, 2002), 44.

8. Stone, *The Biography of Eld. Barton Warren Stone*, 37.

9. Ibid.

10. Ibid., 39.

11. Ibid.

12. Ibid.

13. Ibid., 41.

14. Ibid.

15. Ibid., 34.

16. Galli, "Revival at Cane Ridge."

17. Stone, *The Biography of Eld. Barton Warren Stone*, 37.

18. Ibid., 38.

19. National Back to Church Sunday, "Useful Statistics," accessed January 28, 2016, http://backtochurch.com/participate/resources/statistics/.

20. Pew Research Center, "America's Changing Religious Landscape," May 12, 2015, accessed February 8, 2016, http://www.pew forum.org/2015/05/12/americas-changing-religious-landscape/.

21. National Right to Life, "National Right to Life Issues New Report: 'The State of Abortion in the United States,'" January 21, 2014, accessed February 8, 2016, http://www.nrlc.org/communications /releases/2014/release012114.

22. BBC News, "Islamic State: Egyptian Christians Held in Libya 'Killed,'" February 15, 2015, accessed February 8, 2016, http://www.bbc .com/news/world-31481797.

23. Brian Kelly. "'Their God is My God': Moslem Among the 21 Killed by ISIS Affirms Christ Before Death," Catholicism.org, March 3, 2015, accessed February 8, 2016, http://catholicism.org/their-god-is-my-god -moslem-among-the-21-killed-by-isis-affirms-christ-before-death.html.

24. Twitter.com, "#godloses #lovewins," accessed February 8, 2016, https://twitter.com/search?q=%23godloses%20%23lovewins&src=typd.

24. Michael Brown, "Rob Bell Trashes the Bible on Oprah," CharismaNews.com, February 19, 2015, accessed December 29, 2015, http:// www.charismanews.com/opinion/in-the-line-of-fire/48383-rob-bell -trashes-the-bible-on-oprah.

CHAPTER 3—HOLY FIRE

1. Andrew A. Bonar, *The Works of Rev. Robert Murray McCheyne: Complete in One Volume* (New York: Robert Carter and Brothers, 1874), 217.

2. Hill, *Daily Awakenings*, January 13.

3. James Hamilton, *Works of the Late Rev James Hamilton*, vol. 4 (London: James Nisbet & Co., 1870), 71.

4. David Smithers, "Willam C. Burns," SermonIndex.net, accessed February 8, 2016, http://www.sermonindex.net/modules/articles/index .php?view=article&aid=2543.

5. Bonar, *The Works of Rev. Robert Murray McCheyne: Complete in One Volume*, 82.

6. Islay Burns, *Memoir of the Rev. Wm. C. Burns, M.A.* (London: James Nisbet & Co., 1870), 97.

7. Ibid., 96.

8. Bonar, *The Works of Rev. Robert Murray McCheyne: Complete in One Volume*, 99.

9. J. Harrison Hudson, "Let the Fire Burn: A Study of R. M. McCheyne," The Robert Murray M'Cheyne Resource, accessed February 8, 2016, http://www.mcheyne.info/let-the-fire-burn.php.

10. Bonar, *The Works of Rev. Robert Murray McCheyne: Complete in One Volume*, 82.

11. Ibid., 103.

12. Mark Fackler, "The World Has Yet to See…," *Christian History*, no. 25, posted January 1, 1990, accessed February 8, 2016, http://www.christianitytoday.com/ch/1990/issue25/2510.html.

13. Hill, *Daily Awakenings*, 373.

14. UK Wells, "Robert McCheyne," accessed February 9, 2016, http://ukwells.org/revivalists/robert-mccheyne/.

15. Bonar, *The Works of Rev. Robert Murray McCheyne: Complete in One Volume*, 217.

16. A. W. Tozer, *The Knowledge of the Holy* (San Francisco: Harper-SanFrancisco, 1961), 105–106.

17. Ibid., 104.

18. Bonar, *The Works of Rev. Robert Murray McCheyne: Complete in One Volume*, 205.

19. Ibid., 220.

CHAPTER 4—THE SOUND OF REVIVAL

1. Leona Choy, *Andrew Murray: The Authorized Biography* (Fort Washington, PA: CLC Publications, 2000), 72.

2. Johannes Christiaan Du Plessis, *The Life of Andrew Murray of South Africa* (London: Marshall Brothers, 1920), 190.

3. Ibid., 187.

4. Ibid., 193.

5. Ibid.

6. ReformationSA.org, "Andrew Murray and the 1860 Revival," accessed February 9, 2016, http://www.reformationsa.org/index.php/history/54-1860revival.

7. Lady Duff Gordon, *Letters From the Cape* (London: Humphrey Milford, 1921), 51.

8. Olea Nel, *South Africa's Forgotten Revival: The Story of the Cape's Great Awakening in 1860* (Canberra, Australia: Olive Twig Books, 2010), 103.

9. Ibid., 104.

10. Ibid.

11. Ibid.

12. Du Plessis, *The Life of Andrew Murray of South Africa*, 195.

13. Ibid.

14. Ibid.

15. Ibid.

16. Ibid.

17. Ibid.

18. Ibid., 196.

19. J. D. Kestell, *Het Leven van Professor N. J. Hofmeyr* (Cape Town: Hollandsch-Afrikaansche Uitgewers-Maatschappij, 1911), 92.

20. Du Plessis, *The Life of Andrew Murray of South Africa*, 195.

21. Ibid.

22. Ibid., 195–196.

23. Ibid., 196.

24. Ibid., 195.

25. Ibid.

26. Ravenhill, *Why Revival Tarries*, 17.

27. Ibid., 23.

28. Leonard Ravenhill, "Prayer," accessed February 9, 2016, http://www.ravenhill.org/prayer.htm.

29. Andrew Murray, *With Christ in the School of Prayer* (New York: Fleming H. Revell Co., 1885), vi.

CHAPTER 5—BREAK UP YOUR FALLOW GROUND

1. Charles Finney, *Sermons on Gospel Themes* (New York: Fleming H. Revell Company, 1876), 185.

2. Charles G. Finney, *Memoirs of Rev. Charles G. Finney* (New York: A. S. Barnes and Co., 1876), 99.

3. Ibid.

4. Ibid.

5. Ibid., 100.

6. Ibid., 102.

7. Ibid.

8. Ibid., 103.

9. Ibid., 104.

10. Ibid.

11. Ibid., 105.

12. Charles E. Hambrick-Stowe, *Charles G. Finney and the Spirit of American Evangelicalism* (Grand Rapids, MI: Eerdmans, 1996), 110.

13. Charles G. Finney, *Lectures on Revivals of Religion* (New York: Leavitt, Lord & Co., 1835), 43.

14. Ibid., 44.

15. C. G. Finney, "Break Up Your Fallow Ground," *The Independent*, February 5, 1874, accessed February 9, 2016, http://www.gospeltruth.net/1868_75Independent/740205_break_fallow_ground.htm.

16. C. G. Finney, "God's Love for a Sinning World," *The Obelin Evangelist*, June 22, 1853, accessed February 9, 2016, http://www.gospeltruth.net/1853OE/530622_gods_love.htm.

17. Finney, *Lectures on Revivals of Religion*, 36–39.

18. "Amazing Grace" by John Newton. Public domain.

19. Finney, "Break Up Your Fallow Ground." See also *The Study: Helps for Preachers From English, American, and Continental Sources*, vol. 2 (London: R. D. Dickinson, 1874), 283.

CHAPTER 6—"LORD, BEND US!"

1. Kevin Adams and Emyr Jones, *A Pictorial History of Revival: The Outbreak of the 1904 Welsh Awakening* (Nashville: Broadman & Holman Publishers, 2004), 76.

2. D. M. Phillips, *Evan Roberts: The Great Welsh Revivalist and His Work* (Dolgellau: E. W. Evans, 1912); English translation accessed through D. M. Phillips, *Evan Roberts: The Great Welsh Revivalist and His Work* (Bishop's Waltham: Revival Library Reprints), 170–171; Adams and Jones, *A Pictorial History of Revival: The Outbreak of the 1904 Welsh Awakening*, 43.

3. Roberts Liardon, *God's Generals: Why They Succeeded and Why Some Failed* (New Kensington, PA: Whitaker House, 2003), Kindle locations 1012–1013.

4. Adams and Jones, *A Pictorial History of Revival: The Outbreak of the 1904 Welsh Awakening*, 65.

5. Liardon, *God's Generals: Why They Succeeded and Why Some Failed*, Kindle location 1043.

6. Phillips, *Evan Roberts: The Great Welsh Revivalist and His Work*, 121.

7. Ibid., 90, 120.

8. Ibid., 122.

9. Ibid.

10. Ibid.

11. Ibid., 123.

12. Ibid.

13. Liardon, *God's Generals: Why They Succeed and Why Some Failed*, Kindle locations 1064–1065; see also Phillips, *Evan Roberts: The Great Welsh Revivalist and His Work*, 124.

14. Phillips, *Evan Roberts: The Great Welsh Revivalist and His Work*, 167.

15. Ibid.

16. Ibid.

17. Ibid.

18. Ibid., 186, 211.

19. Ibid., 225–226.

20. Ibid., 211, 225.

21. Eifion Evans, *The Welsh Revival of 1904* (London: Evangelical Press of Wales, 1969), 82.

22. Phillips, *Evan Roberts: The Great Welsh Revivalist and His Work*, 187.

23. Ibid., 194.

24. Liardon, *God's Generals: Why They Succeeded and Why Some Failed*, Kindle locations 1078–1081.

25. Phillips, *Evan Roberts: The Great Welsh Revivalist and His Work*, 194, 217.

26. Ibid.

27. Ibid., 217.

28. Ibid.

29. Ibid., 218.

30. Brynmor Pierce Jones, *Voices From the Welsh Revival, 1904–1905* (n.p.: Bryntirion Press, 1995), 31.

31. Phillips, *Evan Roberts: The Great Welsh Revivalist and His Work*, 218.

32. Jones, *Voices From the Welsh Revival, 1904–1905*, 31.

33. *Western Mail*, "A Wonderful Preacher," November 10, 1904, quoted at "Welsh Religious Revival, 1904," accessed February 9, 2016, http://www.welshrevival.org/histories/awstin1/01.htm.

34. Adams and Jones, *A Pictorial History of Revival: The Outbreak of the 1904 Welsh Awakening*, 99.

35. Elmer L. Towns and Douglas Porter, *The Ten Greatest Revivals Ever* (Ventura, CA: Gospel Light Publications, 2004), 18–19.

36. Phillips, *Evan Roberts: The Great Welsh Revivalist and His Work*, 186.

37. Ken Walker, "Steve Hill: God's Champion for Repentance and Holiness," *Charisma News*, August 23, 2015, accessed February 9, 2016, http://www.charismanews.com/40-year-anniversary/51167-40 -people-who-radically-changed-our-world-rick-warren-steve-hill. See also Michael L. Brown and John Kilpatrick, *The Fire That Never Sleeps: Keys to Sustaining Personal Revival* (Shippensburg, PA: Destiny Image, 2015), Kindle location 404.

38. Phillips, *Evan Roberts: The Great Welsh Revivalist and His Work*, 186.

39. Leonard Ravenhill, "Pentecost at Any Cost," accessed February 9, 2016, http://www.ravenhill.org/pentecostcost.htm.

40. Phillips, *Evan Roberts: The Great Welsh Revivalist and His Work*, 186.

41. Ibid.

42. Ibid., 123.

CHAPTER 7—THE GROUND CRIES OUT

1. Stella Price, *Chosen for Choson: Robert Jermain Thomas* (Essex, MA: Emmaus Road Ministries, 2010), Kindle locations 12–13.

2. Mathew Backholer, *Revival Fire—150 Years of Revivals, Spiritual Awakenings: Days of Heaven on Earth!* (n.p.: ByFaith Media, 2013), Kindle locations 514–515.

3. Price, *Chosen for Choson: Robert Jermain Thomas*, Kindle locations 148–149.

4. M. W. Oh, "The Two Visits of the Rev. R. J. Thomas to Korea," published in *Transactions of the Korea Branch of the Royal Asiatic Society*, vol. XXII (Seoul, Korea: Royal Asiatic Society, 1933), 100.

5. Ibid., 113.

6. Ibid., 112.

7. Ibid., 103.

8. Ibid., 112–113.

9. Ibid., 116.

10. Ibid., 118.

11. Ibid., 119.

12. Ibid.

13. Ibid., 120.

14. Ibid., 119.

15. Ibid., 122.

16. Ibid.

17. Ibid., 123.

18. Backholer, *Revival Fire—150 Years of Revivals, Spiritual Awakenings: Days of Heaven on Earth!*, Kindle locations 556–557.

19. Samuel Moffett, *The Christians of Korea* (New York: Friendship Press, 1962), 53.

20. George T. B. Davis, *Korea for Christ* (New York: Fleming H. Revell Co., 1910), 65.

21. Ibid.

22. Backholer, *Revival Fire—150 Years of Revivals, Spiritual Awakenings: Days of Heaven on Earth!*, Kindle location 504.

23. Ibid., Kindle locations 588–589.

CHAPTER 8—THE CLOUD THAT NEVER LIFTED

1. William Seymour, *The Doctrines and Discipline of the Azusa Street Apostolic Faith Mission of Los Angeles, California* (Pensacola, FL: Christian Life Books, 2000), 46.

2. Frank Bartleman, *How Pentecost Came to Los Angeles* (Los Angles: Bartleman, 1927), 54–55, 60.

3. Cecil Robeck, *The Azusa Street Mission and Revival* (Nashville: Thomas Nelson, 2006), 73.

4. Tommy Welchel, storyteller, *They Told Me Their Stories*, captured in print by J. Edward Morris and Cindy McCowan (Mustang, OK: Dare2Dream, 2006), 41

5. Bartleman, *How Pentecost Came to Los Angeles*, 55, 58–60; see also Robeck, *The Azusa Street Mission and Revival*, 136.

6. "The Millennium," *The Apostolic Faith*, vol. 1, no. 1, September 1906, 3.

7. Ibid.

8. Ibid.

9. Bartleman, *How Pentecost Came to Los Angeles*, 58–59.

10. Robeck, *The Azusa Street Mission and Revival*, 74.

11. Bartleman, *How Pentecost Came to Los Angeles*, 60.

12. Larry Martin, *The Life and Ministry of William J. Seymour* (Joplin, MO: Christian Life Books, 2000), 80, 171.

13. Bartleman, *How Pentecost Came to Los Angeles*, 58.

14. Welchel, *They Told Me Their Stories*, 47.

15. Bartleman, *How Pentecost Came to Los Angeles*, 56.

16. Tommy Welchel and Michelle Griffith, *True Stories of the Miracles of Azusa Street and Beyond* (Shippensburg, PA: Destiny Image, 2013), 32.

17. Bartleman, *How Pentecost Came to Los Angeles*, 38.

18. Ibid., 28.

19. Ibid., 44.

20. Ibid., 60.

21. Welchel, *They Told Me Their Stories*, 50.

22. Ibid., 100.

23. Bartleman, *How Pentecost Came to Los Angeles*, 53.

24. Welchel and Griffith, *True Stories of the Miracles of Azusa Street and Beyond*, 31.

25. Ed Stetzer, "The Real Reason the Pentecostal Movement Keeps Growing," *Charisma News*, February 4, 2015, accessed February 10, 2016, http://www.charismanews.com/opinion/48148-the-real-reason-the-pentecostal-movement-keeps-growing.

26. Robeck, *The Azusa Street Mission and Revival*, 5.

27. "The Same Old Way," *The Apostolic Faith*, vol. 1, no. 1, September 1906, 3.

28. Ibid.

29. Bartleman, *How Pentecost Came to Los Angeles*, 54.

30. Ibid.

31. Seymour, *The Doctrines and Discipline of the Azusa Street Apostolic Faith Mission of Los Angeles, California*, 46.

32. G. B. Cashwell, "Came 3,000 Miles for His Pentecost," *The Apostolic Faith*, vol. 1, no. 4, December 1906, 3.

CHAPTER 9—THEY CAME WITHOUT BEING INVITED

1. Duncan Campbell, "Revival in the Hebrides," audio recording, sermon preached at Viroqua, Wisconsin, May 1968.
2. Ibid.
3. Ibid.
4. "The Hebrides Revival and Awakening 1949–1953," *The Interceders Encourager*, no. 37, accessed February 10, 2016, http://www.call toprayer.org.uk/encourager37.html.
5. Campbell, "Revival in the Hebrides," audio recording.
6. Ibid.
7. Ibid.
8. Ibid.
9. Ibid.
10. Ibid.
11. Ibid.
12. Ibid.
13. Ibid.
14. Ibid.
15. Ibid.
16. Ibid.
17. Ibid.
18. Ibid.
19. Brown and Kilpatrick, *The Fire That Never Sleeps*, Kindle location 358.

CHAPTER 10—GOD IS IN A HURRY

1. Hill, *Daily Awakenings*, September 24.
2. "Amy Elizabeth Ward, 'Mercy Seat,' Alison Ward," *In Times Like These* (Pensacola, FL: Brownsville Assembly of God, August 18, 1995), videotape.
3. Ibid.
4. Steve Hill, "The Miracle at Pensacola," *Awake Now* (Dallas, TX: Steve Hill Ministries, n.d.), videotape.
5. Tim Branson, "Party Teenager Turns to Christ," CBN.com, accessed February 10, 2016, http://www1.cbn.com/700club/party -teenager-turns-christ.
6. Rick Bragg, "In Florida, a Revival That Came but Didn't Go," *New York Times*, May 27, 1997, accessed February 10, 2016, http://www.nytimes.com/1997/05/27/us/in-florida-a-revival-that-came -but-didn-t-go.html.

7. John Kilpatrick, "Revival Stories, Part 2" (Pensacola, FL: Brownsville Assembly of God, 2001), videotape.

8. Steve Hill, "Father's Day Outpouring," *In Times Like These* (Pensacola, FL: Brownsville Assembly of God, June 18, 1995), videotape.

9. Ibid.

10. Ibid.

11. Kilpatrick, "Revival Stories, Part 2."

12. Ibid.

13. Ibid.

14. Hill, "Father's Day Outpouring."

15. Kilpatrick, "Revival Stories, Part 2."

16. Hill, "Father's Day Outpouring."

17. Ibid.

18. "Amy Elizabeth Ward, 'Mercy Seat,' Alison Ward."

19. Ibid.

20. Ibid.

21. Ibid.

22. Branson, "Party Teenager Turns to Christ."

23. Ibid.

24. "Amy Elizabeth Ward, 'Mercy Seat,' Alison Ward."

25. Ibid.

26. Alison Ward, "Brownsville Revival Testimony," YouTube.com, August 18, 1995, accessed January 1, 2016, https://www.youtube.com/watch?v=4aix9SlcLrE.

27. Ibid.

28. Ibid.

29. Ibid.

30. Ibid.

31. Ibid.

32. Ibid.

33. Ibid.

34. "Amy Elizabeth Ward, 'Mercy Seat,' Alison Ward."

35. Richard Crisco, in communication with the author, August 20, 2015.

36. Brown and Kilpatrick, *The Fire That Never Sleeps: Keys to Sustaining Personal Revival*, Kindle location 404.

37. Bragg, "In Florida, a Revival That Came but Didn't Go."

CHAPTER 11—GOD IS NO RESPECTER OF PERSONS

1. Maria Woodworth-Etter, *Acts of the Holy Ghost, and Experience of Mrs. M. B. Woodworth-Etter* (Dallas: John F. Worley Printing Co., 1912), 483.

2. Ibid., 33.

3. Ibid., 36.

4. Ibid., 32.

5. Ibid., 38.

6. "Pentecostal Outpouring in Dallas, Texas," *The Latter Rain Evangel*, August 1912, 10–11.

7. Woodworth-Etter, *Acts of the Holy Ghost, and Experience of Mrs. M. B. Woodworth-Etter*, 352.

8. "Miracles of Healing in Dallas," *The Latter Rain Evangel*, October 1912, 13.

9. Liardon, *God's Generals: Why They Succeeded and Why Some Failed*, Kindle location 3153.

10. Ibid., Kindle locations 4100–4101.

11. Woodworth-Etter, *Acts of the Holy Ghost, and Experience of Mrs. M. B. Woodworth-Etter*, 481.

12. Ibid., 482.

CONCLUSION—THE TRAIL OF FIRE CONTINUES

1. Hill, *Daily Awakenings*, December 16.

2. Leonard Ravenhill, sermon excerpt labeled "Repent Repent Repent," YouTube.com, uploaded January 20, 2012, accessed January 28, 2016, https://www.youtube.com/watch?v=HRNEaSnLsSc.

3. Hill, *Daily Awakenings*, December 16.

CONNECT WITH US!